Mark Hatfield was an importa
time. Now in this well-docun
moral and Christian principl
career, and also shows how such principles might help others to
engage in public service with higher ends in view.

MW00623427

Mark A. Noll

Francis A. McAnaney professor of history,
University of Notre Dame

Mark Hatfield is one of the most significant political figures in
recent memory...significant because he carved out in his day a
creative path between the old options of conservative and liberal.
Because Hatfield was at one and the same time a progressive in
political thought and an evangelical in religious faith, he gives us
today new ways of looking at the interface between politics and
religion. The perspective of Mark Hatfield, as presented in *Stand
Alone or Come Home*, is vital to the contemporary political milieu.

Richard J. Foster

founder of Renováre, and author of various books
including *Celebration of Discipline*

Having spent decades at Mark Hatfield's side, I know this statesman's character to the core. He, indeed, played a historical role in
Oregon's and the nation's political well-being, and is a sorely
missed example in today's acrimonious Congressional halls. All of
his life, Mark Hatfield led his state and country by personal demonstration of faith in God and country. Lon Fendall has captured, in a
superior manner, the spirit and the accomplishments of this talented public servant.

Gerry Frank

former chief of staff to Senator Mark O. Hatfield

Stand Alone or Come Home, which presents Senator Mark O. Hatfield as a disciple of Jesus in the political arena, is a must-read for those who want to understand the role of Christian presence in government. Lon Fendall presents Senator Hatfield as a progressive evangelical whose mission was not to "Christianize" government but rather to bring a Christian understanding of issues into the governmental processes. He sought to be clear on justice and peace in treating all people with equity. From my association (as an inner-city pastor in D.C.), it was evident to me that Hatfield's walk as a disciple and his spirituality of relationship made a special impact on Capitol Hill. As a Mennonite and a pacifist, I am privileged to know and respect Senator Hatfield as my Christian brother.

Myron S. Augsburger

president emeritus and professor emeritus,
Eastern Mennonite University

A generation ago Mark Hatfield modeled Christian political engagement for evangelicals just beginning to think about how to relate faith to politics. Lon Fendall offers an insider's retrospective on a distinguished career in electoral politics. He makes a strong case that Hatfield is comparable to William Wilberforce as a "progressive evangelical" leader, while not hiding the dilemmas and criticisms Hatfield encountered as governor and senator. This book is a timely tool for reassessing the evangelical involvement in public life that has both reflected and contradicted Hatfield's example.

Stephen P. Hoffmann

R. Philip Loy professor of political science,
Taylor University

No matter what you thought of the stands Mark Hatfield took, our nation is richer for his public service. Viewing policy as a deeply moral endeavor and an expression of personal faith, and embracing the common good rather than the advancement of only one party is a pattern we all can follow. This book is an inspiration!

Joel C. Hunter

senior pastor, Northland, Longwood, Florida;
author of *A New Kind of Conservative*

An insightful and accurate portrait of a truly great leader who always endeavored to do the right thing in public policy. One especially important contribution in Senator Hatfield's vast political legacy is the moratorium on U.S. nuclear-weapons testing he achieved in 1992. The moratorium still stands today as the cornerstone of eventually ending the scourge of nuclear weapons worldwide. Many of us working to build on what Mark Hatfield started regard Hatfield as the founding father of progress on the issue we care about most—ending nuclear testing and achieving nuclear disarmament.

Marie Rietmann

former staff to Senator Mark O. Hatfield;
current lobbyist for Women's Action for New Directions
(formerly Women's Action for Nuclear Disarmament)

Stand Alone or Come Home is a significant book about one of the most courageous, biblically faithful, Christian politicians in American history. An important book for anyone interested in applying Christian faith to public life.

Ronald J. Sider

president, Evangelicals for Social Action

Readable, first-rate, inspiring. Lon Fendall tells the inspiring story of Mark Hatfield's career as Oregon's governor and U.S. senator, and of his courageous stands for what were at the time unpopular causes. He clearly shows how these stands—and his progressive approach to public policy issues, more broadly— grew directly out of his Christian commitment as an evangelical. Hatfield's inspiring story is one of Christian faith and commitment to principle overcoming political expediency. I highly recommend this book.

Steve Monsma

research fellow, The Paul Henry Institute for the
Study of Christianity and Politics, Calvin College

Mark Hatfield was an unusual senator from what now seems like a bygone era. But he was simply ahead of his time—a pro-life Republican who was more progressive on social justice and the environment than many Democrats today. Fendall's fine study introduces us to a statesman who fit no type, a Christian with a high view of public office.

James W. Skillen

president, Center for Public Justice

Senator Mark O. Hatfield was one of the most influential evangelical statesmen in the last half of the 20th century. Lon Fendall is undoubtedly correct that his faith had a significant impact on his public service. *Stand Alone or Come Home* is enjoyable history, but it is also a useful guide for Christians as we think about how faith should influence politics in the 21st century.

Mark David Hall

Herbert Hoover distinguished professor
of political science, George Fox University

Every person who aspires to public service should own and use this handbook, which chronicles the humility and courage of a man who was unafraid to stand alone because his principles dictated his politics. Mark O. Hatfield, the modern-day William Wilberforce, is one of the most extraordinary elected officials of the 20th century. His story told by Lon Fendall inspires the reader to consider what American politics could again become.

Tom Getman
executive director international relations,
World Vision International;
Senator Mark O. Hatfield's legislative director, 1978-1985

For more than 35 years Senator Hatfield has been a friend, mentor, and hero of mine. He was gracious enough to write the endorsement for my first book, *Let Justice Roll Down*. His life is a testimony and profile of courage, conviction, and integrity. He had the courage to stand alone as he made the difficult decisions, the right decisions. Everyone could learn from Senator Hatfield's life, and I pray that his example will inspire the next generation of leaders.

John Perkins
founder of John M. Perkins Foundation
for Reconciliation & Development

Fendall does readers a service in pointing to a model for Christians in politics that is framed by the values of human stewardship, reconciliation, and basic human dignity. Hatfield's politics will make interesting reading for a new generation of evangelicals who may be unfamiliar with Hatfield but whose evangelicalism instinctively resembles his.

Timothy Sherratt
professor of political studies, Gordon College

OTHER BOOKS BY LON FENDALL

AUTHOR OF:

Citizenship: A Christian Calling (Barclay Press, 2003)

To Live Free:
William Wilberforce—Experiencing the Man,
the Mission, and the Legacy (Barbour Books, 2007)

COAUTHOR OF:

Unlocking Horns: Forgiveness and
Reconciliation in Burundi (Barclay Press, 2001)

At Home With the Poor: Christian Community
Development in Haiti (Barclay Press, 2003)

Practicing Discernment Together: Finding God's
Way Forward in Decision Making (Barclay Press, 2007)

STAND ALONE
OR COME HOME

Mark Hatfield as
an Evangelical and
a Progressive

by Lon Fendall

BARCLAY PRESS

211 N. Meridian St., #101, Newberg, OR 97132
www.barclaypress.com

STAND ALONE OR COME HOME

© 2008 by Lon Fendall

Published by Barclay Press
211 N. Meridian St., #101, Newberg, OR 97132
www.barclaypress.com

ISBN 978-1-59498-015-2

Cover design by Darryl Brown

CONTENTS

Personal Events

Early years & career in state government

Years in U.S. Senate

1922 Born July 12 in Dallas, Oregon

1925

1930 — Family moved to Salem, Oregon

1935

1940

1943 Graduated, Willamette University; Commissioned as officer, U.S. Navy

1945

Positions in State Government

1948 Masters degree, Stanford University
1949 Joined faculty, Willamette University

1950 Appointed Dean of Students, Willamette University

1950 Elected to Oregon House of Representatives
1952 Reelected to Oregon House of Representatives
1954 Elected to Oregon Senate

1955

1956 Elected Oregon Secretary of State

1958 Married Antoinette Kuzmanich

1958 Elected Governor of Oregon

1960

1962 Reelected Governor of Oregon

	Hatfield U.S. Senate terms	U.S. Presidents	National & World Events
			1963 John F. Kennedy assassinated
			1964 Gulf of Tonkin incident
1965		1963-68 Lyndon Johnson	1965 Protests against Vietnam War become active
1970	1967-72 First term	1969-74 Richard Nixon	
1975	1973-78 Second term	1974-76 Gerald Ford	1973 Roe v. Wade; Watergate hearings; Vietnam Peace Treaty
		1977-80 Jimmy Carter	1978 Jerry Falwell founds Moral Majority
			1979 Iran hostage crisis; Panama Canal transferred
1980	1979-84 Third term		1980 Failed rescue of hostages in Iran
1985	1985-90 Fourth term	1981-88 Ronald Reagan	1986 Iran-Contra scandal; U.S. bombing of Libya
1990		1989-92 George H. W. Bush	1989 U.S. bombing of Libya
			1990 Dissolution of Soviet Union
			1991 First Gulf War
	1991-96 Fifth term		1992 End of apartheid in South Africa
1995		1993-2000 Bill Clinton	1995 Bombing of federal building in Oklahoma City
1997	Retired from Senate		

FOREWORD

My Favorite Senator

I've often said that Mark Hatfield was my favorite U.S. senator. My relationship with Hatfield started when a small group of us were putting together the mailing list for the launch of *The Post-American*, the little tabloid which was the forerunner to *Sojourners* magazine. We were a bunch of rag-tag seminarians in Chicago and our methodology was quite strategic from a marketing point of view. We just sat around in our living room one night and called out the names of people we knew, or knew of, who we thought might like the first issue of this evangelical Christian magazine with a primary commitment to social justice—a new and highly unusual thing in the fall of 1971. As I recall, no other politicians were on our list, but we all admired Mark Hatfield, a U.S. senator and Christian who strongly opposed the war in Vietnam—just as we did.

The cover of the inaugural issue was dramatic: a sculpture of Christ with an American flag wrapped around him above the words, "And they crucified him." The controversial tabloid landed on the desk of Wes Michaelson (now Wes Granberg-Michaelson), Hatfield's chief legislative assistant, and immediately got his attention. After reading it cover to cover, Michaelson walked into the senator's office on a Friday afternoon and told the senator he needed to read it over the weekend. When Hatfield came back on Monday, he told Michaelson to get us on the phone right away because he needed some friends like these young evangelical seminarians, after having received from fellow evangelicals too many letters that began with words like, "Dear former brother in Christ." That was the beginning of my long friendship with one of the most distinctive and principled political leaders of his generation—a progressive Republican who led the fights against both poverty and war, and one of the most outspoken Christians on Capitol Hill.

Over the years, there were many conversations and visits to Hatfield's office and some collaborations I will never forget.

One time, Hatfield called to say he had been invited to give the keynote at the National Prayer Breakfast, the intimate annual breakfast with the president and 2,000 specially invited guests, alwa including many of the nation's most important religious and poli al leaders, along with international dignitaries. The senator asked me what I would say if I were addressing them. It was during the heart of the war in Vietnam, and I told Hatfield I could not write his speech, and he couldn't say what I would say. He said he didn't want me to write his speech; he just wanted me to write what I would say if I were giving the speech. Then he told me I needed to send it to him right away through a new machine called a fax, which used telephone lines—a machine that only the Congress and car dealers had. I wrote what was on my heart to say to the nation's leaders who were prosecuting the war, then went to a Ford dealership in Evanston, Illinois, to send it to the U.S. Senate. We were all watching the evening news the night of the prayer breakfast and Hatfield's speech was the top story on all the networks. He had used the faxed speech almost word for word, and I watched the faces of Richard Nixon and Henry Kissinger as they heard the war in Vietnam called a "national sin and disgrace." I couldn't believe a U.S. senator would do that, but Mark Hatfield would surprise me again and again over the years with a kind of political courage that would often infuriate the powers that be, sometimes in both political parties.

I remember the senator's fervent opposition to the nuclear-arms race. In the face of a SALT II treaty that he thought too weak, Hatfield asked me and Michaelson (who had become one of my best friends and who came to work as *Sojourners* managing editor after he left Hatfield's office) to write an amendment to the treaty calling for a national moratorium on nuclear-weapons production. We wrote the amendment and he put it forward, laying the foundation for the subsequent nuclear-freeze campaign that galvanized millions of Americans against the nuclear-arms race.

One morning during the Reagan era, I saw him on a news show. In a huddle the previous day with fellow Republican leaders as they announced new war plans in Central America, Hatfield looked positively pale and distraught. So I called and left a message that he looked terrible and that if he wanted to talk sometime that week I'd be happy to come over. I got a call an hour later asking if I could come right away. It was one of many precious times when we would retreat to his private office, he'd tell his schedulers not to interrupt, and we would just "kick back" and talk. We would talk about our faith, discuss the meaning of biblical passages, wrestle with complicated ethical issues, sometimes laugh about politics and politicians, and even cry on occasion about the human suffering of war and poverty.

I've known three kinds of political leaders. The first are those who will do the right thing even if it might cost them the next election. The second want to do the right thing if there is enough public opinion behind it. The third just want to get reelected. Most I've known are in the second and third categories. In the first category (which I don't even need both hands to count), Mark Hatfield is at the top of the list. I have never met an elected official who struggled more to be faithful to his principles. Figuring out the right thing to do isn't always easy, but nobody worked harder at it than Hatfield. *Stand Alone or Come Home* describes Mark Hatfield as a unique figure in Washington, D.C.—a political progressive with conservative religious principles, a senator who never fit into the categories of Left or Right, a party leader who wasn't ideologically predictable or reliably partisan, and a dependable voice of conscience in a capital city that often lacks it. I still miss him in Washington, D.C.

I still remember the gleam in his eye and the grin on his face when he first ushered the little group of us from *The Post-American* in Chicago into the Senate Dining Room for lunch, and we were elbow-to-elbow with all the famous senators I had seen on television. I believe he thought he was being subversive. And indeed he often was, the way that a moral conscience always tries to subvert politics.

Jim Wallis
president and executive director, *Sojourners*
author, *The Great Awakening*

PREFACE

The idea for this book has occupied space in my thoughts for a long time. While I felt it needed to be written, I did not feel at all sure that I was the one to do it. One day I mentioned this to someone at a conference in Baltimore. We talked about the distinctive place Senator Hatfield occupied in American politics for nearly half a century and how today's Christians need to hear of his brand of evangelical progressivism. I thought the writer needed to be more objective than I could be as a former Hatfield staff member. The other person disagreed and urged me to start the project.

That night I went to my room puzzling over the challenge. By morning it was clear to me that the book needed to be written—and that I should set out to do it. Understand, therefore, that this book is no dispassionate critique of Mark Hatfield's political legacy; it is instead a personal appreciation for his work and a plea for others to follow his example.

A Few Connections

I first met Mark Hatfield on his home turf in Salem, Oregon. A group of us who held state offices in the Future Farmers of America organization were given an opportunity to meet the governor at the Oregon State Fair in 1959. It was striking to me that even though we felt greatly honored to exchange greetings with the governor, he appeared to feel honored to meet us.

Four years later I met Governor Hatfield again when he came to George Fox College for a chapel interview hosted by members of the "Athenian" student philosophy club. I felt thoroughly intimidated about framing questions for the state's chief executive, but he did his best to put us at ease—and almost succeeded.

A decade later, and in my third year of teaching at George Fox, I wrote to Hatfield asking about a position on his staff. Looking back, I wonder what made me hope I might be hired. After all, I hadn't made the cut a few years before when I applied for a volunteer intern position in his office. And I declined a request to serve as his campaign chairman for Newberg, Oregon, in his 1972 reelection effort. I didn't think I could be effective in helping his candidacy since my schedule was filled with a number of other campaigns at the time.

I gained a little more hope about the political staff work—which at first seemed an unlikely possibility—when I got a call from Hatfield's chief of staff, Gerry Frank. He asked if I was still interested in a staff position and wondered if I could come to his Salem office to talk. Frank's large office intimidated me and I didn't consider my answers to his questions terribly impressive. Still, Frank did his best to put me at ease, even though he could give me no assurance that I would be hired.

In a few weeks I decided to visit Washington to see the senator's office and to try to understand what it might be like to work there. My salary as a junior professor mandated I travel by Greyhound bus—a 36-hour trip from Portland, Oregon, to Washington, D.C. In my short stay in the nation's capital, Hatfield once again made me feel welcome, and I saw one of the many ways he was expressing his faith as he succeeded in getting a resolution passed to declare a national day of prayer, humiliation, and fasting.

I had heard nothing from Gerry Frank about my job prospects by the end of the spring semester at George Fox. Even so, I decided not to sign my faculty contract for the coming year—a step of faith or a foolish choice, depending on one's perspective.

Then during a conversation with a student one day, the phone rang. Frank wanted to know whether I would like to go to work in Washington. And a few weeks later our family—my wife, Raelene; and our two preschool children, Mark and Joyce—was on its way to Washington.

What Lies Ahead

I have had moments of reward and even fun with this book, but also many challenges. I knew from the beginning I wouldn't write a complete biography of Mark Hatfield. But I felt compelled to write this series of biographical essays to explore some of Hatfield's central values and political passions, since his political career and his faith present so many important lessons for us.

I set out to understand and describe one model of political participation that I consider desirable for Christians. Each chapter explores what it means to be an "evangelical progressive" (a label I will define shortly) and Hatfield provides an excellent case study for this political position. Those familiar with his career will soon realize I have selected only those events that fit with this evangelical-progressive theme (and with the parts of his career that I know best).

Identifying Mark Hatfield as an evangelical progressive brings together aspects of his convictions and actions that to some may seem contradictory. As a progressive he occupied an unusual place in the Republican Party. He felt at home in the party of Abraham Lincoln and valued the progressive politics so prominent in the mix of Oregon's political history. Hatfield's form of evangelicalism comfortably blended a born-again spiritual experience, an adamant opposition to abortion, and a commitment to peace and justice. Although the conservative majority of the Republican Party (and of evangelical Christianity) wanted to disown him from time to time, he refused to walk away from either his party or his place in the faith community.

This work explores the meaning and challenges of standing firm against great pressure to conform. And this work tries to stake out space for future evangelical progressives. Hatfield needed to take a stand many times, regardless of the political choices made by others and regardless of pressure from his constituents. This necessity often reminded Hatfield of the counsel his father gave him as a boy—advice given in the context of temptations most likely to dog a young man: "Stand alone, or come home." His father predicted that Mark would find himself in situations where friends clearly intended to do something that was wrong, and his father insisted that in those situations Mark "stand alone, or come home."

Hatfield did take a lonely stand many times in his political career, in some cases literally casting the lone contrary vote. He willingly took the risk of having to "come home" to a career in academia, rather than allow political pressures to drive him into violating his convictions. While his father had in mind taking a stand against inappropriate or unlawful behavior, most often in Hatfield's political career the issue was not misconduct, but pressure aimed at forcing him into a conformity that would violate his convictions.[1]

While this is not a complete biography or even an "authorized" one, Senator Hatfield helped me gain access to some important documentation and helped answer some of my questions. But the interpretations in this book are mine. While I have very deep respect for Hatfield, I have drawn my own conclusions about his work and his character, without checking to see if our interpretations match.

My Gratitude

I am grateful for suggestions from a number of former colleagues on Senator Hatfield's staff, especially Jim Fitzhenry, Gerry Frank, Tom Getman, Wes Granberg-Michaelson, Jim Hemphill, and Janet Lamos.

My association with Hatfield could have never come about if not for my spouse who has been adventuresome regarding our career choices. She supported the idea of applying for a position with Senator Hatfield, even though it required that our family leave the security of a teaching position and move away from extended family and friends to do what we felt God called us to do. I'm delighted to dedicate this book to my wife, loving companion, and friend, Raelene Barnes Fendall.

1

THE EVANGELICAL EXPERIENCE

> I made the choice that night, many years ago: I *committed*
> myself to Christ. I saw that for thirty-one years I had lived
> for self, and I decided I wanted to live the rest of my life for
> Jesus Christ. I asked God to forgive my self-centeredness
> and to make me his own. I was assured by the words of Paul,
> "Therefore if any man be in Christ, he is a new creature: old
> things are passed away; behold, all things are become
> new" (2 Corinthians 5:17).[1]

Senator Mark Hatfield often spoke of his spiritual awakening. Because
he placed so much emphasis on this experience, we ought to understand how it came about and how it affected his life, first as an educator and then as a public official.

Hatfield's description of his spiritual change resonates with
those who have experienced something like it, but often puzzles those
outside the Christian faith or outside the evangelical segment of that
faith. Since some form of this experience typifies evangelical Christians, it seems a logical place to begin. How did Mark Hatfield become
an evangelical Christian, and what impact did spiritual transformation
have on the progressivism that guided his thinking and actions
throughout his career?

A Crucial Phrase

The evangelical vocabulary relating to spiritual rebirth often finds
expression in the phrase "born again." This expression comes directly
from a dialogue between Jesus and a Jewish leader and teacher, re-
corded in the gospel of John.

One night a teacher named Nicodemus came to visit Jesus out of curiosity, skepticism, and fear. Jesus responded with a description of spiritual rebirth. It was impossible, he said, to understand God without being "born again" (John 3:3). The phrase made no sense to Nicodemus and continues to puzzle many people today.

Jesus went on to give the world's best-known summary of the Christian "salvation" experience: "For God so loved the world that he gave his one and only Son, that whoever believes in him shall not perish but have eternal life" (John 3:16). The phrase "born again" means much more than a mere intellectual assent to a few truth propositions; rather, it involves a total reorientation of one's way of living and thinking.

Mark Hatfield heard a great deal of preaching and teaching about spiritual rebirth as he grew up. Since his father, Charles Dolen Hatfield, had a background in the Methodist Church, the family worshiped in a Methodist congregation while living in Dallas, Oregon. Hatfield's mother, Dovie Odom Hatfield, grew up a Baptist, and when the Hatfields moved to Salem, they began attending a Baptist church. Making a personal commitment to Jesus as Savior and Lord was emphasized in both denominations at the time.

Before Hatfield was baptized as a young teenager in the First Baptist Church of Salem, he was expected to give his assent to the Christian faith as defined in John 3:16 and elsewhere in the Gospels. Hatfield credits his father with teaching him what it meant to be a faithful Christian and with setting a godly example. His father diligently studied the Bible and memorized many important passages. Hatfield remembers that his father differed from a good many other railroad workers in that he did not use profanity and he did say a prayer before his meals at work.

Hatfield's mother, too, was far from indifferent about the Christian faith. Both parents considered church participation important. Still, his mother did not believe the church always portrayed accurately what it meant to behave in a way that pleased God. She didn't agree, for example, that being a follower of Christ meant that one had to abstain from dancing, movies, and card playing. In Hatfield's youth many churches considered such activities unsuitable for Christians.[2]

It appears young Hatfield took some cues from his mother in the years after his baptism. While he did not reject the essentials of the Christian faith, he did willingly practice the "vices" his mother found acceptable—and then added a few others, including smoking and (at least in his Navy years) some consumption of alcohol. These practices bothered many members of his church. Interestingly, the same church people also expressed concern when Hatfield began to show an active interest in politics. They taught that Christians should avoid substantial involvement in matters of state; in other words, they held a dualistic view of faith and politics. They insisted that a Christian could and should vote and even speak out on political issues, but to get more actively involved was almost like turning one's back on the faith.[3]

While some considered young Hatfield's behavior wayward, he never rejected his faith. In fact, his superiors in the Navy took note of his faith and called on him to perform some chaplaincy responsibilities during World War II. He did this as a matter of duty and because of his familiarity with Christian practices and theology, though he later faulted himself on the depth of his spiritual life. During his years in graduate study, teaching, and early political participation, many would have described him as a Christian, but not as one passionate about his faith.

A New Beginning

Hatfield's second book, *Conflict and Conscience*, includes a description of his spiritual rebirth. In this and other accounts of his spiritual journey, he speaks of a pivotal experience that profoundly deepened his faith. He likened it to the difference between casually assenting to the principles of democratic participation and becoming deeply involved in public affairs.

Hatfield was urging students in his political science classes at Willamette University to "get down off the bleachers" and get into the game of politics—to take a stand on political questions, to join a party and to help the strongest candidates get elected. He recognized that with respect to his Christian faith, he had been nothing more than a spectator.[4]

Hatfield also became increasingly uncomfortable about the personal counseling expected of him in his role as Willamette University's dean of students. Some students needed simple guidance about their academic and career choices, and he felt comfortable in that role. But others asked him much deeper questions about the meaning of life and whether God existed. Sometimes he dodged these questions by

3

referring students to their pastors, but he became dissatisfied with that approach. He realized students looked up to him and he felt embarrassed that he had little to say about spiritual matters. After all, he was working for a college founded by and with ongoing ties to the Methodist Church. He later called himself as "a-spiritual as they [the students] were a-political."[5]

An important motivator for Hatfield's spiritual introspection came from his contact with a group of students who asked him to sponsor a Bible study. They hoped he would grant university approval for their meetings and he happily agreed to do so. But further contact with these students revealed to Hatfield a spiritual depth and sincerity in them that he lacked. He began to see his spirituality as external, routine, and uncommitted. Their spiritual life seemed deeper than his. He saw it expressed in seriousness about their studies and compassion for others. They *lived* their spirituality, he said, without succumbing to the temptation of self-righteousness.[6]

Among these students, one in particular played a pivotal role in Hatfield's spiritual renewal. Doug Coe also had grown up in the First Baptist Church in Salem. He knew about Hatfield but the two had not become acquainted until Coe asked him for permission to organize the Bible study. Hatfield credits Coe with asking deep questions that pushed him to think deeply about his lack of a vital faith. When Coe asked about Hatfield's religious philosophy, Hatfield couldn't come up with anything more substantial than the Golden Rule.[7]

Troubled by his lack of spiritual resources for counseling students and inspired by the example of these young Christian students who had apparently found some answers, Hatfield came to a turning point in his spiritual life. Midway through the two terms of his service in the Oregon legislature and several years into his service as dean of students (he doesn't remember the exact date), Hatfield made a decision that he claims determined all that he became spiritually. Alone in a room at his parents' home in Salem, he faced the choice between spiritual coldness and spiritual health.

Either Christ is God and Savior and Lord or he isn't, he concluded. If he gave an affirmative answer, he reasoned, then he must do what he had been telling his students to do in regard to political effectiveness—he must make a commitment. He must offer to Christ his devotion, his time, and his very life. Hatfield then made that decision and never looked back.

4

A Rational Decision

Hatfield didn't speak of this renewal experience as his being "born again." Why? For one thing, his decision was rational and unemotional, nothing like the "emotional high" experienced by some who "accept Christ" in evangelistic meetings.

For some believers, emotions pour out over deep anguish regarding horrible sins. They feel compelled to repent of grievous wrongdoing; the conversion experience of the apostle Paul is a biblical example. Hatfield, however, had not felt guilty about grossly sinful behavior; instead he struggled with feelings of emptiness and spiritual inadequacy. And he had no emotional struggles over making a new and deeper spiritual commitment; he simply gave rational assent to Christ as his Lord and Savior. In fact, when he made the choice he wondered if by the next morning he would think he had done something silly.[8]

A Remarkable Answer to Prayer

Doug Coe's account of his interaction with Hatfield at this time gives Hatfield considerable credit for Coe's own spiritual awakening. Although Coe had grown up in the church, he struggled spiritually after high school and ultimately left the church. Although he rededicated himself as a Christian during his sophomore year at Willamette, he wondered if God really answered prayer. So he decided to set up a three-month "experiment."

Coe wrote down some specific prayer requests without telling anyone about them. If there really was a God who answered prayer, Coe reasoned, then he should see some specific answers to these prayers. It was after he began this experiment that Coe went to Hatfield to ask him to authorize the use of a room for a Bible study.[9]

After that encounter, Coe decided to add Hatfield to his prayer list. He reasoned that if Hatfield were to experience a spiritual awakening, it would prove there was a God who answers prayer. Within the three months Coe had allotted for his prayer experiment, Hatfield called Coe into the dean's office. Like any undergraduate getting called into an administrator's office, Coe assumed he was in trouble. Coe guessed that Hatfield felt upset about some critical comments Coe had made about the lack of spiritual depth in the Willamette chapel services.

Instead, Hatfield asked Coe if he would drive with him to a meeting in Corvallis. During the forty-five minute trip, Hatfield told Coe that he had decided to fully commit his life to Christ. He hadn't told anyone yet and he hoped Coe would understand and support his decision. Coe felt utterly amazed that Hatfield would confide a major decision like this to him, a mere student. More amazingly, here was the "proof" he sought that God answers prayer. Coe felt so shocked at Hatfield's disclosure that he couldn't think of how to respond.[10]

The next day Coe went to see Hatfield to apologize for not offering more affirmation at the news of Hatfield's spiritual rebirth. In that exchange, Hatfield asked Coe to pray for him. Coe said he didn't feel comfortable praying out loud, especially for a university official. So Hatfield prayed for Coe. This time together established a spiritual bond that became very important to both men. Coe's doubts about God vanished with this dramatic answer to prayer, and Hatfield began to consider Coe a confidant on spiritual matters.

Hatfield and Coe began to meet regularly for prayer and discussion, sometimes late at night, since both had such busy schedules. Occasionally Hatfield invited Coe to accompany him on speaking trips so they could talk. Coe marveled at Hatfield's voracious reading of the Bible and other Christian literature and Hatfield felt impressed with Coe's spiritual intensity.[11]

A Progressive Role Model

An English politician whose career spanned the 18th and 19th centuries had a spiritual rebirth experience that, in some respects, foreshadowed Hatfield's. As a boy, William Wilberforce heard the preaching of some evangelical ministers, including John Newton. These preachers emphasized spiritual rebirth and faithful obedience to Christ, in contrast to the less "radical" form of Christianity practiced in the Church of England. John Wesley had significantly influenced these evangelicals through his emphasis on personal salvation by faith, along with attentiveness to the evils of society. But Wilberforce's family made a point of squelching his interest in evangelicalism in favor of the much more socially acceptable Church of England.

The family's resources and social position got Wilberforce admitted to Cambridge University, but by his own account he did almost no studying there. After his election to the House of Commons at age twenty-one, Wilberforce served in Parliament with no substantial political or personal goals. Then he encountered a Christian who challenged him to rethink his dismissal of the theology and spirituality of the evangelicals. With minimal nudging from this friend, Wilberforce made the same kind of rational, unemotional commitment to Christ that Hatfield would make many years later. Such a commitment profoundly affected the lives and political careers of both men.[12]

After Hatfield later encountered the writings of Wilberforce, he wrote an introduction to a new edition of Wilberforce's book *Real Christianity*. Hatfield noted the similarity of their spiritual rebirth experiences and said that he had modeled his life after Wilberforce without being conscious of the fact.

It is worth noting the parallels between the experiences of these two Christian politicians, since such an examination sheds light on Hatfield's spiritual and political development. Wilberforce worked for more than 20 years within Parliament to enact a ban on the slave trade in the British Empire. Then he worked for another 26 years for the complete abolition of slavery in Britain and its colonies, a much larger task that did not end successfully until he lay on his deathbed.

Wilberforce enjoyed the assistance of a group of evangelicals who often met at an estate in Clapham for inspiration, mutual encouragement, and strategy. Wilberforce worked with these evangelicals and with Quakers on a number of other social justice and evangelical causes.[13]

Hatfield and Wilberforce both struggled with the implications of making their new faith in Christ known in public venues. Both had established their reputations in politics without being identified as evangelicals and both wondered if this new identity would become a political liability. For Wilberforce, continuing as a token Christian within the Church of England would have been politically safe; for Hatfield, downplaying his new spiritual experience and keeping any reference to it out of his public discourse would have been prudent. There was and is a prevailing notion of separation of church and state that calls into question any public references to personal spiritual experiences.

Both Hatfield and Wilberforce engaged in serious, private study of Scripture and prayer after committing their lives to Christ. Both gradually left behind some of the practices in which they had engaged,

THE EVANGELICAL EXPERIENCE

such as drinking and smoking. And each reached a point at which they felt they must "go public" to be true to their new faith.

Wilberforce had a more difficult time publicly declaring his faith than did Hatfield. The British member of Parliament (MP) had risen to a position of significant national prominence, in large part because of his close friendship and political alliance with Prime Minister William Pitt. With considerable hesitation, Wilberforce made known his new evangelical faith to Pitt, expressing the possibility that faithfulness to Christ might oblige him to step out of politics. Pitt urged him not to think of his new faith as incompatible with his political career and predicted they could still be allies, even if their lifestyles diverged.

Wilberforce also struggled with the idea of going to John Newton, a person of lower social status, to seek spiritual counsel. For Wilberforce, it seemed like a point of no return. What would happen if he openly associated with a well-known evangelical minister like Newton?

As it turned out, Wilberforce's new identity as an evangelical did not hurt him politically and in fact brought him many allies in the struggle against slavery.[14]

Hatfield did not share Wilberforce's wonderment about the compatibility of becoming an evangelical Christian and staying in politics. Despite the questions some in his home church raised about his desire to go into politics, he proceeded with this choice of career after his spiritual awakening. He later articulated the clarity of his sense of being called into politics:

> For the Christian man to reason that God does not want him in politics because there are too many evil men in government is as insensitive as for a Christian doctor to turn his back on an epidemic because there are too many germs there. For the Christian to say that he will not enter politics because he might lose his faith is the same as for the physician to say that he will not heal men because he might catch their diseases.[15]

But Hatfield wondered, as Wilberforce had, about the political consequences of making explicit public references to his renewed faith in Christ. Fortunately, by then he had the benefit of regular spiritual discussions and prayer with Doug Coe. Coe encouraged him to accept invitations from Christian groups who wanted to hear about his faith experience, reasoning that this would provide a relatively unthreatening venue in which to begin talking about such things. And in fact, many of those who heard Hatfield talk about his faith affirmed his experience and promised to pray for him.

The harder question for Hatfield was whether he should talk about his new spiritual experience in broader settings such as service clubs, farm groups, and educational institutions. People had begun coming to Hatfield to ask that he pray for their personal needs and he felt comfortable doing so, but this was not the same as making public statements. For a time he decided to say nothing in public venues about his faith. Then he became more courageous and began to say, "God bless you" in his speeches, a relatively innocuous form of publicly expressing his faith.

Hatfield and Coe each have a different memory regarding the first time Hatfield made more than innocuous references to God in his public appearances. In Hatfield's memory it occurred at an event in the state's capital city, Salem. Although the Christian youth organization Young Life had sponsored the event, the dinner attracted a number of state leaders and its very location made it a media event. Hatfield knew that many in attendance would prefer that politicians limit their faith statements to the private arena. And he also knew that some attendees were people of faith but not Christians—such as those of the Jewish faith—and they certainly would not share his view of Jesus Christ. He recalled being struck with a painful headache as he talked about his faith, feeling the stress of the possible consequences for doing so.

Coe, on the other hand, points to a speech Hatfield gave in eastern Oregon—on the topic of Oregon's economy—as the first time Hatfield was specific about his faith in Christ. Hatfield did not intend to refer to his faith, he told Coe later, but at the end of his talk he adlibbed that Oregonians would be better off if they took God more seriously and that they could know God through Jesus Christ. On the way home, Hatfield told Coe he shocked himself that he had made the statement and he speculated about the political fallout. He hoped the main newspapers in the state wouldn't hear what he had said in a location so far from Salem. As it turned out, the *Oregon Statesman* mentioned his comment in a subtitle to its story about his talk. But few critics took issue with Hatfield's first public expressions of faith (as was the case for Wilberforce). Rather, a growing number of individuals commended Hatfield for his public witness and sought him out for prayer and counsel.[16] From that point there was no question of turning back toward a private Christianity.

A Christ-Empowered Faith

Hatfield has never downplayed the faith experience that proved so central to the man he became, both as a person and as a politician. It might have felt tempting at times to disassociate himself from the religious and political conservatives who felt drawn to him because of his faith, for many of these Christians assumed that religious conservatism could not be separated from political conservatism. When Hatfield took progressive and liberal political positions, many of these supporters loudly questioned his standing as a Christian.

This questioning became particularly intense during Hatfield's growing opposition to the Vietnam War. In the face of severe attacks on his politics and his faith, Hatfield did his best to make decisions consistent with his conscience and his efforts to obey Christ. *(We will explore the many questions raised by conservative Christians about Hatfield's opposition to the Vietnam War in chapters 8 and 9.)*

In 1971, facing a difficult reelection effort in the Senate, Hatfield reiterated the centrality of his Christian faith in his book *Conflict and Conscience*:

> Following Jesus Christ has been an experience of increasing challenge, adventure, and happiness. How true are his words: "I am come that they might have life, and that they might have it more abundantly" (John 10:10). It is not to a life of ease and mediocrity that Christ calls us, but to the disciple-like, Christ-empowered life. No matter what field we are in, we are called to give our complete allegiance to him. No cause, noble as it may seem, can be satisfying or purposeful without the direction of Christ. I can say with all sincerity that living a committed Christian life is truly satisfying because it has given me true purpose and direction by serving not myself, but Jesus Christ.[17]

While being an evangelical meant a number of things to Hatfield politically, he saw his faith primarily as a spiritual experience—as a living relationship with Christ.

2

EVANGELICALISM
AND PROGRESSIVISM

Christians who heard of Hatfield's newly invigorated faith thought they could understand that part of him reasonably well. When he spoke of his determination to "follow Christ," they recognized his decision as a very important part of his personal experience. The problem arose with the associations often made between *evangelical* faith and *conservative* politics.

As earlier noted, evangelicalism for someone like William Wilberforce in 18th-century England meant a blend of conservative theology with a determination to rid society of its many social evils. For Wilberforce the social evil was slavery. But in the 1950s, when Hatfield began his political career, many who heard the term *evangelical* did not connect it with its historical origins. They did not consider it a progressive response to society's needs and therefore had difficulty understanding Hatfield's mix of theological and political ideas.

Walter Russell Mead, senior fellow at the Council on Foreign Relations and an influential writer on issues of U.S. foreign policy, wrote an article in 2006 called "God's Country." He classified Christians in the United States as fundamentalists, liberals, and evangelicals, acknowledging the fluid boundaries among the groups. He placed evangelicals in a middle position between fundamentalists and liberals. In many ways his evangelical label corresponds to the evangelical progressive position we have ascribed to Mark Hatfield. Yet while Mead's categories may usefully describe the role of Christians in public policy in the early 21st century, they don't serve as well for the period spanned by Hatfield's political career.[1]

A True Evangelical?

Tony Campolo asserts that to be an evangelical simply means believing in orthodox Christian theology as expressed in statements such as the Apostles' Creed, along with adhering to a high view of the Bible and experiencing some form of spiritual rebirth.[2]

Hatfield expressed these evangelical principles in a prayer he gave at the 1969 Presidential Prayer Breakfast. These gatherings have a broadly ecumenical tone and many who give addresses there use the inclusive language of "faith in God," hoping to avoid offense. But Hatfield included in his prayer several references to the need for human hearts to be purged of sin, the centrality of loving Jesus Christ as Savior, and the guidance and protection of the Holy Spirit. His vocabulary and his personal experience clearly identified him as an evangelical.[3]

No one has ever dismissed Hatfield as an evangelical based on the faith propositions he embraced. His experience of spiritual renewal also aligns with the experiential side of the evangelical profile. So what is the problem in understanding Hatfield as an evangelical? The questions that arose always related to the assumption that being an evangelical is a mismatch with progressive political positions.

Many in the evangelical community add a conservative political creed to Campolo's formula. These individuals assume that not only is there a measure for theology and experience, but also a political template for evangelicals. True evangelicals, they say, must believe that welfare is bad, the rhetoric of civil rights is questionable, war is necessary, support of the president is required (particularly when he or she is a Republican), and free enterprise is next to godliness.

Mark Hatfield took stands completely contrary to parts of this conservative creed. And so his evangelical critics—without bothering to scrutinize his theology or his faith experience—often rushed to exclude him from the evangelical camp. Some, in fact, wondered if they would see him in heaven. Hatfield wouldn't score zero on a conservative evangelical checklist, but his politics frequently did not line up with many of the politically conservative evangelicals.

Shortly after the 1973 *Roe v. Wade* decision on abortion, Hatfield adopted a "pro-life" stance, a position that became central to conservative ideology in the ensuing years *(see chapter 12)*. Many times Hatfield's positions on public policy questions reflected his caution about relying on the federal government to solve all human problems, a caution typical of conservatives. Even though many conservative Christians appreciated Hatfield's views on these points, they expected him to agree with them on *all* the tenets of their conservative ideology. When he didn't, they wondered if he were truly "one of them."

A "Flaming Liberal"?

Whenever Mark Hatfield spoke to evangelical audiences, some in the audience were bound to feel puzzled over how he applied his faith to politics. When he addressed a commencement audience at Fuller Theological Seminary in 1970, for example, he urged graduates and guests to reclaim the social witness of their gospel message and reattach it to their emphasis on personal evangelism. In effect, he implored them to claim the 18th century form of evangelicalism practiced by William Wilberforce and his associates.

Hatfield also asked his Fuller audience to set aside the "unacknowledged alignment of conservative Protestantism with conservative social and political interests."[4] He expressed these progressive ideas despite the fact that he had heard how some of Fuller's donors had complained to the president about the seminary inviting a "flaming liberal" to speak there. What could have been an icy reception, however, turned into a warm endorsement.[5]

But many evangelical Christians, both in Oregon and around the nation, expressed far less acceptance of Hatfield's ideas than did the audience at Fuller. They regularly let Hatfield know they considered his unique mix of evangelical theology with progressive ethics both inappropriate and unacceptable. And often they expressed those views in unkind ways.

At one point Hatfield discovered his staff had been keeping from him the most hostile of the letters he received from constituents. He insisted that he be allowed to receive the full measure of indignation expressed in the letters, as hard as that was.

While one can find examples of these attacks throughout Hatfield's career, those expressed in the late-1960s and early-1970s seem particularly intense. In most cases, the writers were upset about

Hatfield's outspoken opposition to the Vietnam War. Very often the criticism assumed that an evangelical should support the president, particularly when that president exercised his function as commander in chief of the armed forces.

One such letter addressed Hatfield as a "former brother in Christ," and asserted he couldn't possibly be a follower of Jesus since he didn't support President Nixon, who (according to Romans 13) had God's support and blessing. Another writer said Hatfield omitted from his theology an appreciation for the evil in human nature.

Many of these letters were addressed directly to Senator Hatfield, but others went to the editors of various Christian publications, claiming that Hatfield's stand on the war provided ample evidence that he could not be a real Christian.

In later years critics wrote letters to Christian magazines calling Hatfield's concern for the poor and hungry of the world "the same old socialist blah" and a contradiction of the biblical assertion that poor people would always have a place in the world. "Our first charge from the Lord Jesus," said one reader of *Moody Monthly*, "is to preach the Gospel. There is no other command to feed the world."[6]

Voters in Oregon, especially Hatfield's fellow evangelicals, expressed similar concerns in person during the senator's trips to Oregon. Some of those at one particular event threatened to discourage and embarrass both the senator and those who invited him. For years Hatfield had gone to the Conservative Baptist "Men's Roundup" to give a Sunday morning devotional talk and biblical exposition. Although he never discussed political issues during these spiritual retreats and had no intention of doing so when he went in 1970, some attendees prepared to use the occasion to express their distaste for his position on Vietnam. They planned to walk out in protest before he could even begin speaking. Such a display would be painful for Hatfield because the Conservative Baptist churches were his own branch of the broader Baptist movement. These were his people and those who had invited him had always shown gratitude for his willingness to speak there.

When told in advance about the protest plans, Hatfield expressed his disappointment and with some reluctance agreed to cooperate with the leader's strategy for sidetracking the walkout. Instead of giving an introduction immediately before Hatfield spoke, the leader gave the introduction, then immediately led in prayer, having prompted Hatfield to come to the platform during the prayer. As the leader expected, the group planning to exit the hall was caught off guard and decided against staging their protest during prayer. Before they could decide what to do, Senator Hatfield had begun his talk and the protest ended before it began. Despite the tactical victory, the incident offered an unpleasant reminder that many in Oregon did not understand the senator's form of evangelical progressivism.[7] But it was during this time Hatfield began to understand that he had company in his position.

What's a Progressive?

In 1971 a staff member showed Hatfield the first issue of a new Christian periodical called the *Post American* and encouraged him to read it. The publication would have alarmed an evangelical more conservative than Hatfield, but Hatfield read the magazine with great interest.

While the periodical's founders embraced a completely evangelical theology, they also clearly shared the senator's political convictions. The editors insisted that those of an evangelical faith must apply their theology to society's need in ways not always aligned with conservatism. Hatfield told one of the magazine's editors, Jim Wallis, that he couldn't agree more that Christians had to base their obedience to Christ upon Christ's teachings, rather than accept prevailing assumptions about a Christian's rightful position on politics and social issues.[8]

At Hatfield's invitation, Wallis became a regular visitor to the senator's office, especially after 1975 when the publication moved its offices to Washington, D.C., and changed its name to *Sojourners.* Hatfield agreed to become a contributing editor, "going public" with his endorsement of the magazine's expression of evangelical progressivism. The magazine's staff members felt delighted with Hatfield's warm encouragement, and he in turn felt pleased to find kindred spirits. He hoped that the credibility of the evangelical progressive position, as explained and defended within the pages of the magazine, might gain more support for the position among evangelicals in general.[9]

Hatfield developed a political position that was much like what Wallis has since identified as a "progressive and prophetic vision of faith and politics."[10] The term *progressive* seems more appropriate to describe Hatfield than the term *liberal*, since Hatfield did his best to

EVANGELICALISM AND PROGRESSIVISM

develop positions that fit his own convictions, rather than try to fit into any doctrinaire orthodoxy (whether liberal or conservative). The "progressive" label also helps explain Hatfield's ideas to that segment of the population unfamiliar with Christianity, who may feel puzzled by Hatfield's seeming contradictions. *(We will explore some historical and political dimensions to the "progressive" label in chapter 3.)*

On a political continuum from liberal to conservative, "progressive" is seen as closer to the liberal side than to the conservative side. But liberals frequently took exception to Hatfield's views, for he seemed just as willing to depart from a strictly liberal agenda as he did from the conservative creed. The typical political labels do not work well when speaking of Hatfield. But the *progressive* term seems to be the most useful one in characterizing his political stands.

The Senator's Alter-Ego

A young man named Wes Michaelson (now Wes Granberg-Michaelson) had a part in making the connection between Hatfield and Wallis. Michaelson was a young volunteer when he first met Hatfield at the 1960 Republican Convention in Chicago. Michaelson recognized this political newcomer—still in his first term as Oregon governor—as both an impressive political leader and an emphatic evangelical.

Michaelson connected with Hatfield again in early 1968 at a workshop associated with the Presidential Prayer Breakfast. By then Michaelson had begun to search for ways to apply his theological studies at Princeton Seminary to the political and social issues of the day, especially the Vietnam War. Michaelson commended Hatfield for his courageous stand against the war and asked if he might be able to work in the Hatfield office to fulfill his seminary field-experience requirement. Hatfield agreed and Michaelson went to work as an intern on a modest stipend.[11]

Michaelson, encouraged by Jim Wallis and other young evangelical progressives, came to occupy a unique role on the staff with respect to Hatfield's developing evangelical progressivism. Wes learned how to shape the words that formed the basis for many of Hatfield's pivotal speeches. That meant working long hours on causes he found very fulfilling, but it also meant postponing his completion of seminary.

An indication of Michaelson's influence on Hatfield's thinking can be found in one of Michaelson's major writing projects, Hatfield's 1976 book, *Between a Rock and a Hard Place.* The book differed substantially from Hatfield's two previous books. The first, *Not Quite So Simple,* came about in part through the efforts of one of Michaelson's predecessors on staff who also had an interest in Vietnam—Gayle Osburn DeBruyn. Hatfield published the book in 1968 as he looked for ways to express his convictions about Vietnam and to connect those convictions with his evangelical progressive views. The next book, *Conflict and Conscience,* came out three years later. This collection of speeches and essays provides helpful insights into Hatfield's thinking during his first term in the Senate, but doesn't give a systematic window into that thinking.

In introducing *Between a Rock and a Hard Place,* Hatfield gave credit to Michaelson, his principal collaborator on the book, even calling him his "alter ego." That was not an exaggeration. By the time the two finished the book, they had been collaborating on oral and written material for six years.

Hatfield worked with many fine staff members in Oregon politics and during his early Senate years, and many others influenced his thinking after the Michaelson era. But no one before or after Michaelson had more influence with regard to the place Hatfield staked out for himself as an evangelical progressive.

Between a Rock and a Hard Place did not enjoy great sales success, especially when compared with sales figures for other books aimed at a Christian audience and released at around the same time. Its publisher, Word Books, had a primary market among evangelical readers and many who read the book still had not come to terms with the validity of the evangelical progressive position. One reviewer gave the book faint praise, calling it "one of the most unusual pieces of political literature in American history." Another reviewer said Hatfield seemed better at naming problems than proposing solutions. Several evangelical magazines put it on their list of significant books of the year, but beneath the surface of the reviews there was a good deal of puzzlement about the place Hatfield occupied among the small group of evangelicals in national politics.

Competing at the time with Hatfield's book for both evangelical and general readers was Charles Colson's *Born Again.*[12] The public remained curious about Colson's role in Watergate and fascinated with the faith experience of Nixon's "hatchet man." Colson's book was long on story with little deep theological reflection, while Hatfield's readers had to engage challenging biblical exegesis and serious historical and theological content. It is no small task to work through the competing Christian views on "just war" and pacifist theory, starting from the early days of Christianity! But Hatfield tried to do just that, with Michaelson's help.

Kindred Spirits in the Senate

Apart from the assistance and affirmation Hatfield received from staff members for his evangelical progressive position, one fellow senator shared many of his spiritual and political values. Harold Hughes, a Democrat from Iowa, became Hatfield's closest ally in the Senate on a spiritual, theological, personal, and political level. While Hatfield felt comfortable sharing friendships and engaging in worship and Bible study with fellow senators John Stennis and Sam Nunn—despite their dramatically different positions on several key issues—no one approached Hughes as Hatfield's closest confidant.

Hughes became an early ally in opposing the Vietnam War, readily agreeing to co-sponsor the McGovern-Hatfield amendment to terminate funding for the Vietnam War. Hughes also shared Hatfield's commitment to the poor of the world and his respect for human life that led to a pro-life position on abortion. When Hatfield felt deeply discouraged about the stinging opposition coming from conservative Christians, Hughes was one of his few peers whom he believed would fully understand. Together they struggled with how to impact public policy and how best to defend their views among constituents who neither understood nor agreed.

As a Democrat, Hughes didn't face as many conservatives such as those who insisted Hatfield had become a renegade Republican. Still, most of Hughes's constituents in Iowa were just as rural and conservative as the people of Oregon. The two senators endured many of the same criticisms from evangelicals and wished that voters could demonstrate more trust in their personal faith experiences when sharp political differences arose.

Unfortunately for Hatfield, Hughes decided in 1973 not to run for reelection, instead choosing to answer what he considered a higher calling to address issues concerning alcoholism. When Hughes left the Senate, Hatfield greatly missed the collegiality and fellowship the two had experienced.[13]

Other Allies

Several others helped Hatfield solidify his position as an evangelical progressive in the early years of his political career. One was Doug Coe, the Willamette University student to whom Hatfield had first confided his newfound evangelical faith.

After graduating from Willamette, Coe began organizing breakfast gatherings hosted by political leaders at every level of government—especially mayors, governors, members of Congress, and the president. Along with sponsoring these annual public events, Coe and others organized small Bible study groups and one-on-one interaction between ordinary citizens and prominent leaders. His movement also arranged gatherings among peers from different settings and from various parts of the world. This prayer breakfast movement has successfully provided a loosely-knit network for spiritual nurture without becoming publicly prominent.

The Hatfield-Coe relationship resembled those among other participants in the prayer breakfast movement. Coe never advised Hatfield on political issues and never sought political favors. They were friends and spiritual brothers and Hatfield felt confident he could openly speak to Coe about the political and personal issues that impacted his spiritual and emotional well-being.

Long before their encounters in Washington, Hatfield consulted Coe while trying to decide about proposing marriage to Antoinette Kuzmanich, a Catholic of Croatian descent and an educator at Portland State University. In the mid-1950s when Mark and Antoinette began dating, many Protestants had serious difficulties with the idea of "intermarriage" with Catholics, as if the two faiths were not both part of Christianity. Coe counseled Hatfield not to worry about the stigma conservative Protestants had placed on "mixed marriages" and his reassurances helped to keep the Hatfield marriage plans moving forward. Mark Hatfield married Antoinette Kuzmanich on July 8, 1958, and eventually the couple reared two sons and two daughters.

Coe was also encouraging to Hatfield in 1973 when Hatfield pondered how to formulate his remarks for the Presidential Prayer

Breakfast, which came at a time of distress in his relationship with President Nixon. Coe counseled Hatfield to speak as the Holy Spirit directed and not to worry about the president and others misinterpreting his message. This was one of several cases where Coe urged Hatfield to remain faithful to his convictions, to continue as he felt led.[14]

Hatfield found another spiritual counselor and friend in Richard Halverson. When the Hatfields moved to Washington, D.C., and purchased a home in Bethesda, Maryland, they began attending Fourth Presbyterian Church in Bethesda. Halverson pastored that church, eventually serving for 23 years.

Hatfield chaired the Senate Appropriations Committee in 1981 when the Senate appointed Halverson as chaplain; the senator had much to do with the appointment. The Hatfield-Halverson relationship consisted largely of warm friendship and Christian fellowship, nurtured by regular meetings for prayer and mutual encouragement. The relationship felt comfortable for both men, in part because Halverson made a point of never pushing his views on legislative proposals. Rather, Halverson saw himself as a friend and pastor to members of both parties and looked for ways he could encourage and pray for them. Halverson typically began his meetings with Hatfield by saying, "Mark, how may I pray for you?"

While Halverson might not have shared Hatfield's strong anti-war agenda in the early 1970s, the pair agreed that compassion for the world's needy was part of the Christian's privilege and responsibility. Halverson served for a time on the board of World Vision, as Hatfield did, and both men insisted that evangelicals needed to find better ways of responding to the needs of the world's poor. Halverson affirmed Hatfield's evangelical progressivism and served as his spiritual mentor and anchor throughout his Senate years.

Halverson's close ties to Hatfield and other evangelicals in the Senate allowed him to move comfortably through the Senate chambers, meeting rooms, and offices. Like Hatfield, Chaplain Halverson became best known for his interest in and compassion for the many staff people in the Capitol. When it came time to give the opening prayer each day, he prayed meaningfully and graciously. He carried out his pastoral ministry primarily behind the scenes as an encourager and friend to the members of the Senate and the thousands of staff on Capitol Hill who kept the place going. And he contributed greatly to Hatfield's spiritual steadiness and his ability to deal with the challenges of his growing seniority and power in the Senate. While in a position of some influence himself, Halvorson continued to emphasize the qualities of servanthood and humility so central to the character of Jesus.[15]

The Decision about Running for Reelection

Hatfield began *Between a Rock and a Hard Place* with a story about a conversation he had with Wes Michaelson in 1971 as they drove together to the airport for yet another trip to Oregon. Hatfield talked about his frustrations with public life and declared that if he were to decide then, he would not run for reelection.

Hatfield had plenty of reasons for discouragement. Summer heat, humidity, and smog in the nation's capital made the idea of moving back to Oregon look very appealing. He had tried repeatedly with Senator McGovern and other Senate allies to get a measure passed that would have ended the war. Meanwhile, in spite of his efforts to communicate with his Oregon constituents, the message he heard when he visited Oregon was not always positive. Some complained that he was not responding to their letters very promptly and helpfully. Others complained that he was not visiting their community often enough and wondered if he was too busy with foreign policy issues to care about their needs. Polls showed that he would probably lose if he ran for reelection the following year. He felt ready to hang it up.

Michaelson knew his boss well enough to absorb his discouragement and to assure him he would support a decision not to stay in politics. While it would have disappointed Michaelson if Hatfield were to leave the Senate (as Harold Hughes would soon do), Michaelson understood the need for considering the possibility that the senator might need to "come home," having stood alone so many times in state and national politics.

Hatfield's private pondering about running for office continued for months, for the decision was about more than the odds of winning the election. Could Hatfield remain faithful to his convictions as an evangelical progressive while serving in public office? That was the core issue. And to understand that issue we must examine the unusual place Hatfield occupied in the Republican Party of his day.

3

A REPUBLICAN PROGRESSIVE

Most people think of evangelicals as loyal and conservative members of the Republican Party. Mark Hatfield was indeed a loyal Republican, but not a conservative in most respects. As stated earlier, some observers at the time found this hard to understand, and many continue to wonder about it.

While Hatfield struggled with the policies and values of Republican presidents, especially Richard Nixon, he never gave much thought to abandoning his party. His boyhood political heroes were all Republicans and every campaign he won, he won as a Republican. When his critics asserted he showed disloyalty to Republican principles, he insisted that the party had room for progressives as well as for conservatives. In fact, for Hatfield, Republicanism had a long history of progressivism. But most party leaders disagreed, and more than once Hatfield chose to "stand alone" when they tried to push him into the conservative mainstream of the party. Hatfield dealt with those pressures as best he could, while remaining loyal to his party both while in office and afterward.

Choosing a Party

How do people choose a political party? Political scientists have researched that question and have decided that most individuals choose their parents' political party, often without giving the matter much thought.[1]

But what if one's parents belong to different parties, as in the Hatfield family? While Hatfield's mother, Dovie, was a loyal and outspoken Republican, his father, Charles, was an equally loyal Democrat. Each parent influenced Hatfield in different ways.

By Hatfield's account, his mother's independence of thought and expression ran way ahead of her time. She was a feminist before most people knew what the term meant; still, she remained a loyal Republican. While she was away from home during the weekdays getting her teaching credential at Oregon State College in Corvallis, Hatfield's father served as the on-site parent. So it might be said that Hatfield inherited his progressivism from his father's Democratic values and his loyal Republicanism from his mother.

During his first legislative campaign, Hatfield jokingly applied some guilt tactics to his father's choice of party. He suggested that if his dad didn't switch parties, the lack of his vote might keep Mark from winning the election. (In Oregon's "closed primary," voters receive a ballot listing only their registered party's candidates.) The friendly pressure paid off and the senior Hatfield changed his registration so that he could vote for his son. Hatfield won the nomination and the family remained united (in the partisan sense) from that time forward.[2]

Despite their differing party loyalties, Hatfield's parents completely agreed in their mutual distaste for the philosophy and policies of President Franklin D. Roosevelt. Hatfield recalls how anti-Roosevelt rhetoric unified political discourse in his home.[3] It was his mother's passion for partisan politics that influenced him to choose the Republican Party.

A Loyal Republican in Hard Times

If Mark Hatfield were to be judged by his ability to pick winning presidential candidates, his early record would seem quite unimpressive. He clung to his Republican sympathies even when Republicans made a poor showing against Roosevelt's enormous popularity in the 1930s and 1940s.

In 1936 Hatfield passed out campaign buttons for Alf Landon. When Landon's running mate, Frank Knox, came to Salem for a brief campaign stop, the fourteen-year-old Hatfield joined the party faithful at the train station. Despite Landon's poor performance as a campaigner, Hatfield knew the *Literary Digest* had predicted a Landon victory, so he wagered seven milkshakes on the Republican candidate. Landon's defeat cured young Hatfield of relying on political polling and also on betting on the outcome of an election.[4]

It didn't, however, cure Hatfield of backing Republicans. The 1940 candidacy of Wendell Wilkie had a particular attraction to Oregonians. Wilkie and the party had picked a popular Oregon politician, Charles McNary, as the vice-presidential nominee. McNary had served as dean of the law school at Willamette University, and since 1917 had won an uninterrupted series of U.S. senatorial contests. The Republicans staged a public event in Salem, featuring McNary's nomination as vice president. Thousands of Oregonians showed up at the fairgrounds in Salem to express their support for the Wilkie-McNary ticket. Businesses proudly displayed McNary campaign material and some of them closed their doors so employees could attend the rally.

Of course, eighteen-year-old Hatfield joined the crowd, cheering for the hometown hero. If he hadn't got hooked on Republican politics prior to that, his addiction got a major fix at the McNary event.[5]

Hatfield's enrollment at Stanford University in a political science graduate program solidified his preferences for the Republican Party. He knew that Herbert Hoover, a Republican president, was one of Stanford's first and most successful graduates. And it was Hoover whom Hatfield chose to study for his master's thesis.

After Hatfield left Stanford he became an instructor at Willamette University, where he taught a class dealing with the role of political parties. While he waited for political opportunities to present themselves within the Republican Party, he volunteered to speak on behalf of the Hoover Report. This document advocated restoring power to the Congress and the courts—power that its supporters felt had been lost during the Roosevelt presidency. Speaking about the document gave Hatfield his first public exposure in a variety of venues in Marion County (whose largest town, Salem, also served as the state capital). This involvement opened doors for Hatfield's entry into Republican politics, first as state chairman of the Young Republican Policy Committee, then as precinct committeeman, and then as an officer in the county central committee of the party.[6]

The Roots of Hatfield's Progressivism

It would be a mistake to assume that Hatfield began his career as an orthodox, conservative Republican and only later moved in a more progressive direction. In fact, Hatfield's early positions on domestic politics were anything but conservative.

Consider the following progressive positions adopted by the Young Republican group that Hatfield chaired in 1949:

- providing more adequate assistance to the elderly and poor
- restoring water quality
- taxing the timber industry to generate funds for forestry research
- putting an end to racial discrimination.

Hatfield advocated these issues, and others equally on the progressive side, in his first campaign for office a year later.[7]

Those who fail to note Hatfield's early progressive positions could be misled in part by a distorted impression of Herbert Hoover, Hatfield's political hero. Hoover's defeat in 1932 during a time of national and global depression resulted in his lasting reputation as a passive, uncompassionate, even inept president. Hatfield didn't see Hoover in that way at all.

At age six, Hatfield could not take part in the successful 1928 Hoover presidential campaign. But four years later, he helped the Hoover campaign by distributing campaign material around his neighborhood in his coaster wagon.[8] And through the years Hatfield invested time and effort toward promoting an image of Hoover as a compassionate and progressive leader. Some recent Hoover scholarship attributes Hoover's difficulties not to a lack of commitment to relieving human suffering, but to shortcomings in his political and relational style.[9]

As Hatfield constructed his own progressive political philosophy, he drew many of his progressive ideas directly from Hoover. Hatfield cited Hoover's book *Challenge to Liberty*, published in 1934, as an important source for his political commitments, such as compassion, open-mindedness, and equal opportunity for those willing to work. Hatfield eventually adopted a form of political progressivism often called "classical liberalism," as distinguished from the kind of liberalism championed by Franklin Roosevelt. Roosevelt went far beyond Hoover's concepts in shaping federal policies. In part, it was Roosevelt's political skill that forged the enduring negative image of Hoover as a man who cared only about the wealthy while ignoring the needs of the poor and hungry.[10]

Hatfield also considered his progressive ideas to be rooted in the pre-Hoover history of the Republican Party. As Hatfield saw it, the party was born out of concern for an oppressed group, the slaves, and the party found its original strength in the restoration of their person-hood, dignity, and economic opportunities. He believed Republicans to be well-positioned to apply such progressive ideals to a variety of needy individuals in the mid-20th century: owners of small businesses, blue-collar workers, the urban poor, and those who struggled to make a living on farms.[11]

A significant thread of progressivism in early Oregon politics also contributed to Hatfield's political philosophy. While in recent years Oregon has earned a decidedly progressive reputation, this ethos has always coexisted with its conservative ideology. During Hatfield's boyhood years the Ku Klux Klan still had an active presence in Oregon, and remnants of such groups still linger today. Nevertheless, Oregon's progressive reputation has a solid base in the state's early adoption of several critical tools for popular participation in decision-making: the initiative, the referendum, and the recall. These mainstays of the national progressive movement opened the way for the flourish-ing of grass-roots democracy that lasted throughout the twentieth century.

As he formed his political views, Hatfield realized that Oregon had become a national leader in other progressive positions, such as women's suffrage, child-labor laws, worker benefits, and the progres-sive income tax. He saw no incompatibility between these views and his affiliation with the Republican Party.[12]

On to the National Party Convention

National party conventions bring excitement into the lives of the po-litically faithful, and Hatfield's first chance to participate in the presi-dential nominating process came in 1950 soon after he first won elec-tion to the Oregon House of Representatives. At that time, Republicans were searching for a strong candidate to challenge the Democratic stranglehold on the White House. So Hatfield began working on behalf of the candidacy of the popular and winsome Kansan, Dwight D. Eisenhower, even though the general had no experience in politics and had not even declared his party preference.

Three things had to happen in order to get Eisenhower's name on Oregon's primary ballot in May 1952. First, supporters needed to collect a thousand signatures on a nominating petition, a task party workers soon accomplished. Second, Eisenhower needed to register as a Republican, which he did in 1952. Third, Eisenhower had to announce his candidacy in time to gain a spot on the Oregon ballot, which he also did.[13]

On that same primary ballot, Oregon Republicans had to choose delegates to the national convention. Hatfield became one of ten at-large delegates, which enabled him to carry his support for Eisenhower to the party's convention. Before the proceedings began, the Oregon delegates caucused and elected Hatfield to the platform committee, giving him an opportunity to support the Eisenhower candidacy from this strategic location.

A Shift to the Right

While Hatfield's political leanings aligned well with early Republican progressive politics, many Oregonians in the 1950s joined other Americans in a shift toward the political right—just as Hatfield got his start in politics.

Senator Joseph McCarthy of Wisconsin began his crusade to identify and expose "Communist sympathizers" in the State Department and elsewhere, in both the public and private sectors. His accusations fell on the fertile ground of fear, fertilized by the rising strength of the Soviet Union and a perception of the waning power of the United States. The fact that Hatfield did not drift into such anticommunist extremism can be attributed to his progressive political foundations.

A young and inexperienced candidate would have found it difficult in some states to win a first election without obtaining the active support of his or her party, but Hatfield had no such trouble. He welcomed party support when he first ran for the legislature, but he also realized he needed to recruit an independent, bipartisan cadre of supporters. As he later said, "People aren't Democrats or Republicans, they're people." Accordingly, he and his early advisor and strategist, Travis Cross, designed and built a "people to people" campaign, based on recruiting respected leaders in every community, regardless of their party. Instead of approaching only the most likely backers of Republicans, he sought the support of anyone who seemed sympathetic, regardless of the person's party or political profession.

Hatfield's success in recruiting supporters from among Democrats and Independents helped him a great deal in 1956 when he got ready to run for his first statewide office, secretary of state. Because he had already built a broad coalition of support, he could continue crafting his own mix of progressivism and conservatism—a mix that appealed to Democrats and Independents, as well as to moderate and progressive Republicans. He could, for example, talk to voters in the middle and on the left about his successful sponsorship of legislation to ban racial discrimination in Oregon's public places, such as restaurants and hotels. The major newspaper in the state, *The Oregonian,* endorsed Hatfield for secretary of state, calling him one of the "enlightened" younger Republicans, one "worthy of support outside his own party."[14]

To further attract a wide range of voters, Hatfield sought and obtained labor support—an unusual accomplishment for a Republican. In 1952 he accepted an invitation to present his case to union members at the Labor Temple in Salem and walked away with the endorsement of the Teamsters, support he retained in every subsequent election. A good many Teamsters were seasonal cannery workers who during the rest of the year labored on their family farms, so their views were not as faithful to Democratic orthodoxy as other union members. After 1957, when the government prosecuted national Teamster official Jimmy Hoffa for obstruction of justice in a case that associated him with organized crime, Teamster support might have become a liability, but labor leaders in Oregon had not been involved with these national scandals.

In his final Senate race, Hatfield nearly won the endorsement of Oregon's largest labor organization, the American Federation of Labor and Congress of Industrial Organizations (AFL-CIO). By then he could talk to union members about jobs he had helped bring to Oregon through a variety of federally-funded projects.

Building his own political organization also gave Hatfield the freedom to appoint Democrats to prominent campaign positions, symbolic of the support he sought and received outside his own party. He maintained cordial relationships with Democrats in the Oregon congressional delegation, so when he asked them to accept honorary positions, many willingly did so. Representative Edith Green endorsed Hatfield in 1984 and Congressman Robert Duncan did so in 1990. Significantly, Duncan agreed to give his support even though Hatfield had defeated him in the 1966 election.

Opposition From Within and Without

Not surprisingly, Hatfield's courtship of labor and Democratic support annoyed many Republican loyalists. Moreover, some felt he had climbed the political ladder too rapidly and had not given sufficient respect to mainstream Republican traditions and principles. Many felt pleased when he began talking more openly about his born-again faith and lifestyle, but others expressed discomfort with such statements offered in the public arena. Hatfield quit smoking and no longer frequented the "smoke-filled rooms" where party leaders and lobbyists built relationships and negotiated deals.

Hatfield also encountered resistance to his brand of progressive Republican politics at the national level. After he successfully worked to get civil rights legislation passed in Oregon while serving in the legislature, it seemed important to him to pursue similar efforts nationally. At the 1961 governors' conference in Hawaii he introduced a civil rights resolution that drew strong opposition from both conservative and moderate governors. The moderates, though sympathetic, insisted that trying to adopt a civil rights resolution would divide the governors and ultimately delay progress on the issue. The following year Hatfield renewed his efforts on the civil rights issue, supporting the progressive Republican governor Nelson Rockefeller of New York in an unsuccessful attempt to overcome the resistance of Southern governors.

Civil rights became an even more contentious matter at the 1963 governors' conference in Miami. Hatfield and other Republican progressives tried to outmaneuver Southern governors to pass a civil rights resolution. Ironically, enough northern Democratic governors gave their support to the Southerners, which effectively sidetracked progressives' efforts. Opponents eventually succeeded in abolishing altogether the resolutions committee of the conference, thus eliminating the normal pathway toward consideration of this kind of measure.[15]

Despite these behind-the-scenes clashes with the conservative mainstream of his party, Hatfield emerged into the national spotlight at the 1964 Republican National Convention in San Francisco. He took his turn as one of a rotation of presiding officers—and then, quite remarkably, party officials picked *him* to deliver the keynote address.

Why should party leaders—who expected Barry Goldwater to win the nomination—pick someone like Hatfield to give the keynote? After all, Hatfield's values bore little resemblance to Goldwater's. One reason had to do with Hatfield's considerable success in Oregon politics, having moved quickly from the Oregon House of Representatives, to the Oregon Senate, to secretary of state, and then to the state's chief executive position. Hatfield had other assets as well: Longtime loyalty to the Republican Party, an impressive military record, confidence and effectiveness as a public speaker, and considerable attractiveness and warmth in the new medium of television.

Hatfield had one glaring liability, however—one that convention planners either did not fully consider or decided to overlook. Anyone examining his legislative actions and speeches could not have failed to see his progressive convictions and policies. Goldwater should have known what was coming, for Hatfield had given a speech in Goldwater's home state in 1963 in which he scathingly denounced the right wing of the party, whose positions he said threatened racial and religious minorities.[16] At the time Hatfield gave the keynote address, however, the Goldwater nomination had not yet been secured and backers of Governor Nelson Rockefeller would have found more to admire in Hatfield's progressivism than in Goldwater's "pure" conservatism.

Hatfield's speech at the Cow Palace carried the title "A Program of Faith," and those who hoped for an affirmation of mainstream Republicanism found some encouragement in several of its points. Hatfield spoke in favor of the bedrock values of the party: capitalism, free enterprise, anticommunism, and democracy. He spoke of the importance of religious values as a basis for American democracy. But the

A REPUBLICAN PROGRESSIVE

conservative majority at the convention became restless when Hatfield moved on to express his concern about defending the rights of American citizens against racism and hatred. "There are bigots in this nation who spew forth their venom of hate," he said. "They parade under hundreds of labels, including the Communist Party, the Ku Klux Klan and the John Birch Society."[17]

Hatfield intentionally included the John Birch Society on his list of bigoted organizations, even though he knew there were supporters of the group scattered around the convention hall, most notably in the large California delegation. As if to annoy these conservatives even further, Hatfield spoke of the need for compassionate assistance to the nation's hungry and its elderly poor—certainly not topics designed to bring cheers from Goldwater supporters.

Conservatives got an even greater jolt when Hatfield staked out new territory in opposition to U.S. involvement in Southeast Asia. Of course, in doing this Hatfield was criticizing Democrats in the White House, and usually it's considered fair game to criticize the policies of the other party at one's own convention. Even though Eisenhower had started the United States on a pathway to involvement in Southeast Asia, presidents Kennedy and Johnson had pushed this initiative much more aggressively than had the Republicans. But who expected Senator Goldwater to take a *less* aggressive role in Vietnam than President Johnson had? Conservatives found Mark Hatfield's foreign policy rhetoric profoundly disturbing. His keynote statements on Indochina *(discussed in more detail in later chapters)* threw down the gauntlet before party conservatives.[18]

Had a trapdoor existed behind the speaker's lectern, members of the program committee probably would have pushed the button and brought a speedy end to Hatfield's address. Interestingly, one measure of the unpopularity of the speech actually did involve the speaker's platform Hatfield stood on. As Hatfield gave his speech, his personal driver—an Oregon State police officer—crawled under the platform to check for a bomb, since someone had called in a bomb threat.

A few courageous liberals among the delegates, such as Senator Jacob Javits of New York and Senator John Sherman Cooper of Kentucky, cheered Hatfield's remarks, as did the Oregon delegation. But the overall response ranged from cool to downright hostile. Keynote speakers rarely elicit boos from their audiences, but the hall's most

STAND ALONE OR COME HOME

conservative delegates gave Hatfield exactly that treatment. Accordingly, no one from the Goldwater campaign later called on Hatfield for his support.[19]

A Friend of Nixon

We will later delve into the drama of the 1965 and 1966 national governors' conferences, when Hatfield emerged into national leadership of the anti-Vietnam War movement. Despite his position on Vietnam, Oregon's voters elected him to the U.S. Senate in 1966. And two years later, Richard Nixon seemed to give serious consideration to Hatfield as his vice presidential choice. But why?

Nixon's interest in Hatfield resulted in part from the warm friendship that had been growing for several years. The pair met when Hatfield participated in his first Republican convention, where Eisenhower picked Nixon as his vice-presidential running mate. In 1958 Nixon backed Hatfield in his first campaign for governor, calling him one of the great hopes for the Republican Party and one of the party's outstanding young leaders. Nixon telephoned his congratulations after Hatfield's victory and not long afterward the vice president visited Oregon to represent Eisenhower at Oregon's centennial celebration. While in Oregon, Nixon had lunch at the Hatfield home and thereafter never failed to praise Mrs. Hatfield's cooking. Nixon also came to Oregon to campaign on Hatfield's behalf during Hatfield's 1966 Senate race.[20]

Taking into account their friendship, Nixon arranged a meeting with Hatfield in June 1968, to discuss the senator's possible support for Nixon's candidacy. In the light of Hatfield's tepid reception as Republican Convention keynoter in 1964 and his unwillingness to join other Republican governors in 1965 and 1966 to endorse the Vietnam War, one might wonder why Nixon would value the support of an "outlier" in the party. But Nixon had no assurance of winning the nomination over the popular moderate Republican, Governor Nelson Rockefeller of New York—and getting the backing of another moderate Republican, such as Hatfield, would provide him with a strategic advantage.

With the benefit of historical hindsight, the greater question is not why Nixon might want Hatfield's support, but why Hatfield would agree to give it, which he indeed did. Fortunately, Hatfield explained his reasoning a few weeks later in an article in *Christianity and Crisis* titled "Richard Nixon for President." Hatfield also announced and explained his decision in a news conference after meeting with Nixon. In both venues, he made the following points:

- Vice President Hubert Humphrey made it very clear that he would continue the Johnson war program in Vietnam—the least desirable potential outcome of the election, from Hatfield's perspective.

- Hatfield and other Republican senators met with Governor Rockefeller during the spring and specifically asked him about Vietnam. Hatfield felt very disappointed in Rockefeller's response and believed Rockefeller would continue the Johnson-Humphrey pursuit of the war. Moreover, Rockefeller's foreign policy advisor, Henry Kissinger, appeared likely to push Rockefeller in a hawkish direction. (This point now seems ironic, in the light of Kissinger's crucial foreign policy role in the Nixon administration.)

- Hatfield believed Nixon understood that the war had less to do with combating communism in Asia than it did in finding a way to respond to the economic and humanitarian needs of the Vietnamese people.

- Hatfield and Nixon agreed that an all-volunteer army would provide a far superior system than continuing the draft.

- Nixon had not yet announced his position on the Vietnam War and Hatfield thought he had a better chance to influence that policy as a supporter than as an outside critic.[21] This was probably the most important point.

Up to the time of Nixon's death, Hatfield consistently pointed out that Nixon deserved a reputation as one of the brightest politicians of modern times. In fact, during their interactions of June 1968, Nixon's intellect and craftiness may have gained him the advantage over Hatfield. Nixon promised only to *consider* Hatfield's position if Hatfield would pledge his support—more than Hatfield thought he could gain from other candidates. Later events made it appear that wishful thinking had clouded Hatfield's judgment, but this did not seem so obvious in June 1968. In any event, Nixon went into the nominating convention with the benefit of Hatfield's support.[22]

Apart from his private discussions with Nixon, Hatfield landed on the short list of vice-presidential candidates for some of the same reasons he had been asked to keynote the party convention in 1964. Despite the unpopularity of that speech among party conservatives, even Hatfield's critics conceded that he made a good impression in his public appearances and that he had an impressive list of political victories. Hatfield was one of a group of attractive and moderate young Republican senators; others included Charles Percy of Illinois, Howard Baker of Tennessee, and Edward Brooke of Massachusetts. Hatfield spoke increasingly before Christian audiences, where—by 1968—he earned a reputation for his sincerity.

Nixon decided that he wanted a running mate who could credibly step into the presidency—someone who could campaign effectively and who agreed with his views. This final point alone should have disqualified Hatfield as Nixon's vice-presidential choice. No one active in national politics could have remained unaware of what happened at the governors' conferences or of the prominence of Vietnam in Hatfield's Senate campaign. And it was no secret that Hatfield had expressed support for the only antiwar candidate in the primaries, Democrat Eugene McCarthy. But few at the time knew that Hatfield had been approached to enter the New Hampshire primary as a peace candidate before McCarthy decided to do so.[23]

While Nixon had not declared his position on the war prior to the Republican convention, few doubted he would ultimately support the war. While publicly remaining neutral on the issue, Nixon privately sent the message to Hatfield that the senator's stand on the war might make it awkward to pick him as a running mate.[24]

While discussions on the vice presidential choice took place behind closed doors, party officials asked Hatfield to give a seconding speech on behalf of Nixon's nomination. They clearly knew of Hatfield's announced support for Nixon and hoped that the senator's progressive positions could win support for Nixon among delegates who agreed with Hatfield, especially on the need to seek peace in Southeast Asia and on the importance of faith in public life. In short, party officials wanted Hatfield to "deliver" the peace votes and the religious votes.

Hatfield found himself in a difficult position as he prepared his remarks for the convention. As he said privately to Nixon's campaign manager, John Mitchell, he felt as though he knew Nixon well from their personal interactions, but didn't know much about his political beliefs or his faith experience. Mitchell suggested that Hatfield talk about the Quaker faith of Nixon's mother. Hatfield responded that talking about Nixon's religious heritage wouldn't be likely to impress the delegates, unless her values clearly characterized Nixon himself.

Hatfield also asked what he could say that would sound compelling to delegates eager to end the war in Vietnam. The private assurances Nixon had given Hatfield earlier no longer seemed so persuasive. Mitchell replied that Nixon did indeed intend to get the United States out of Vietnam, but when he could provide no details, Hatfield felt bewildered about how to proceed. Hatfield went ahead to speak in support of Nixon as he had agreed to do, but always considered it a difficult experience.[25]

Republicans left the convention after choosing Richard Nixon as their presidential candidate, having passed over Nelson Rockefeller, Ronald Reagan, and a handful of "favorite sons." As the delegates left the hall, they passed television monitors that showed Nixon assuring them the party could unite behind his candidacy and that he had made no deals regarding his vice-presidential choice.[26]

A news story in the *Miami Herald* that day announced prematurely that Hatfield would be Nixon's choice, but no such decision had been made. Nixon had promised to consult with delegates from every region before he made his decision; clearly he had no intention of picking someone unacceptable to Southern party leaders, however, and one of the stronger voices among those delegates belonged to Strom Thurmond.

Thurmond, a U.S. senator from South Carolina who had converted to the Republican Party in 1964, felt angry about the headline in the *Miami Herald*, not because he disliked Hatfield, but because it demonstrated that the South had not been fully consulted on Nixon's choice. Thurmond had promised to gather support for Nixon from Southern delegates as a first step in what would become the "Southern strategy"—a strategy that helped Nixon gain the votes of 692 delegates, more than double the count for Rockefeller. In exchange for his efforts, Thurmond understood he would have a voice (or even a veto) in the Republican's vice-presidential choice. Certainly he wouldn't have picked Hatfield, who had championed civil rights throughout his career and whose views on Vietnam clashed with those of the typical conservative Southerner.[27]

The public, of course, knew nothing about these behind-the-scenes efforts of Thurmond and other Southern delegates. When the convention recessed early Thursday morning, the media was still guessing who might be picked. ABC assigned Peter Jennings to cover events at Hatfield's hotel, in the event he would be chosen. A handful of Hatfield's friends and staff members spent most of the night developing contingency plans in case he would be asked to serve and in case he decided to accept. But Hatfield demonstrated his own ambivalence about the issue when he decided to go to bed instead of staying up for the strategy session.

Hatfield got a little sleep, but a series of phone calls interrupted his rest that night. The first two came from his friend (and an informal advisor to Nixon), Christian leader Billy Graham. Graham called from the Nixon suite in the Hilton Plaza where the decision would be made. In the first call Graham assured Hatfield of his full support and indicated the senator might be chosen, but in his second call Graham reported that someone else had been picked. Herbert Klein, Nixon's press secretary, called soon afterward to assure Hatfield that he was still under consideration. Some time later Klein called again to give the final word: Hatfield was not the choice.[28]

The Hatfields left the convention to spend time with friends just as officials announced Spiro Agnew as the vice presidential choice. Hatfield left with mixed feelings about his consideration for the vice presidency. He had devoted his career primarily to politics, so the possibility of becoming second in line to the White House had some appeal.

On the other hand, the Hatfields knew that the rigors of a national campaign and subsequent travels on behalf of the president would have taken Hatfield away from his young children more than he would have liked. Hatfield fully realized that his selection was a long shot and that it could put him in a serious struggle between his antiwar convictions and the necessity of remaining loyal to a president who might carry on with the Vietnam War.

Hatfield later recalled that while he felt some excitement over his possible selection, he also knew that if he became the choice he would have had little choice but to tone down his rhetoric on Vietnam.

That requirement would have presented its own difficulties, since he had risked so much during his Senate campaign with his antiwar position.

Republican Opposition in Oregon

Hatfield's tenuous relationship with national party leaders during his first term in the Senate eventually became an issue for the party in Oregon. When in January 1970 President Nixon nominated G. Harrold Carswell for the Supreme Court, Hatfield lined up with Carswell's critics, noting the judge's weak judicial record and poor stand on civil rights.

Hoping to persuade Hatfield to vote for the confirmation, a group of Oregon Republicans sent the senator a telegram urging his support and threatening to cut off their support if he failed to do so. Their ill-advised pressure tactics had the opposite effect they intended, for Hatfield soon went public with his opposition to Carswell.[29]

Later that first term the chair of the Oregon Republican Party, Peter Gunnar, publicly expressed his disapproval of Senator Hatfield's stand on Vietnam. When Hatfield announced his plans to run for a second term, state party leaders responded with tepid support. In some states this would have proven politically fatal, but the strength of Hatfield's own support network meant that he didn't need a lot of help from state party officials to proceed with an effective campaign.

In 1972 Oregon Republican leaders hoped that Hatfield's Republican loyalty would permit him to overlook his differences with Nixon on Vietnam and support the party's presidential ticket, a logical thing to expect. But Hatfield remarked early in 1972 that he felt unsure Nixon and Agnew *should* be nominated again. This was too much for Irv Enna, then the state GOP chair, who told a reporter that Hatfield's uneasiness about Nixon and Agnew was reason enough for Hatfield to consider leaving the party and joining the Democrats.[30]

If Hatfield had followed Enna's suggestion, it wouldn't have marked the first time a major political figure in Oregon had switched parties. Senator Wayne Morse had spent many years in politics before he left the Republican Party in 1952, identified himself as an Independent for two years, then moved to the Democratic Party in 1955. But for Mark Hatfield to leave the Republican Party would have been as unlikely for him as leaving the Baptist Church. While he had plenty of differences of opinion with his Baptist friends in Oregon, he never thought seriously of changing denominations. And Hatfield considered his identity as a Republican nearly as embedded in his own values as he did his commitment to his denomination.

Hatfield's response to Enna's suggestion was that he had known Enna for a long time and was disappointed that Enna would make such a suggestion. He added that public officials and private citizens had a duty to oppose positions taken by their party (and especially their party's president) that they considered clearly hurtful. He considered that he was doing President Nixon a favor by pointing out the negative consequences of continued military involvement in Southeast Asia.[31]

Many Oregon Republicans withheld their support for Hatfield through the years, though most party leaders and citizens consistently backed the senator despite their personal differences on Vietnam and other questions. The typical mainstream Republican leader in Oregon who couldn't agree with Hatfield simply stayed in the background and let the senator run his own campaigns and continue his own process of communicating with his constituency. But Walter Huss, a very conservative Oregon Republican and outspoken fundamentalist Christian, was one exception.

Huss decided in 1966 to run against Hatfield in the Republican primary for the U.S. Senate, but had little experience and credibility to mount a serious challenge. In subsequent years, Huss persuaded many conservative Republicans—many of them active Christians, like Huss—to seek and win election as precinct committee persons, county precinct officers, and state party officials. This grassroots takeover of the party had such success that Huss's followers eventually elected him statewide party chairman.

During Hatfield's 1978 general election campaign, Huss took public exception to Hatfield's statement that major cuts could be made in the defense budget without jeopardizing national security. Hatfield normally refrained from responding to critics if he felt they lacked credibility, a tactic he typically used with Huss. But Hatfield responded to Huss by reiterating his view that much of the defense spending was wasteful and excessive. He also expressed surprise that Huss, a conservative minister, seemed to place his trust more in the gods of militarism and materialism than in the God of justice and peace.[32]

Restoring Goodwill

Despite his clash with Huss, Hatfield remained on good terms with most leaders of his own party. When differences arose with GOP colleagues, he acknowledged the differences and sought to restore goodwill.

Even when he found himself standing alone among Republicans, Hatfield never seriously thought about changing parties. He embraced the view that a party should have flexible boundaries that welcomed debates between ideological and tactical rivals.

Hatfield defended his brand of progressive Republicanism on historical grounds, and insisted the party would be stronger as it welcomed progressives and liberals, along with conservatives, into the party. As he grew accustomed to those who questioned his rightful place in the Republican Party, he also learned to deal with the scrutiny he received as an evangelical in public life. We turn in the next chapter to his efforts to keep his actions in line with his faith commitment.

4

WALKING THE TALK

Evangelicals believe that following Jesus produces changed behavior. But to what extent should an evangelical politician's convictions shape his or her conduct—both public and private? How does the personal conduct of Mark Hatfield speak to this often-asked question?

Personal Faith, Public Behavior

Some individuals inappropriately restrict evangelicalism to a list of behavioral taboos—something like the legalism of the Pharisees in the Gospels, only with a different set of sinful behaviors. Jesus went out of his way to reject such legalism, teaching instead a broader ethical system based on acting consistently with one's love for God and other humans.

Evangelical progressivism asserts that the implications of personal faith in Jesus go beyond issues of personal behavior. Mark Hatfield advocated for such an ethical system, informed by his Christian faith and his broader moral orientation. He argued that what a person did about the moral imperatives of compassion, peace, justice, and service mattered as much as, or even more than, what a person did in his or her "personal life"—relating to such issues as sexual conduct and substance use.

Hatfield believed that congruence between one's personal and public behavior *mattered*. A person who publicly advocated a certain lifestyle should not privately live in a manner contrary to that public persona. He did not agree with his peers who claimed that their performance in public life had no connection to their personal conduct;

Hatfield insisted that since private behavior might embarrass family and much of the public, it mattered. Yet while he maintained that one needed to live uprightly, he never argued that acceptable personal conduct was *in itself* a sufficient measure of the Christian ethics.

More than Abstention

In his boyhood home, Hatfield was blessed (or cursed) by a sharp divergence between his parents' views on certain behavioral standards and those typical for the churches his family attended. The First Baptist Church in Salem, which the family joined, held theological and lifestyle views representative of Baptists and other evangelicals of the time.

The church held to something like a two-tier system of "forbidden behaviors." On the upper tier were sexual misconduct, alcohol consumption, and tobacco use. On the next tier were activities such as dancing, attending movies, gambling, and playing cards. With the possible exception of compulsive gambling, evangelicals today would not label this second tier of behaviors "sinful," but most Baptists and other evangelicals in the 1930s and 1940s—when Hatfield was growing up—considered all these things unacceptable.

Hatfield's mother, however, challenged the second-tier sins. While in his student days and while in the Navy, Hatfield himself indulged in the first-tier sins of consuming alcohol and smoking. Although these habits never appeared to become addictions, the people of his church frowned on these behaviors, as noted later by one of his church peers.[1]

Hatfield deemed these prevailing views of Christian ethics distorted. It seemed to him that many churchgoers considered the Christian faith to be nothing more than abstaining from a long list of sinful behaviors. By refusing to abide by these moral constraints, Hatfield allowed himself to be considered a non-Christian by some churchgoers, but it didn't seem to him that being a Christian meant only that one abstained from a list of banned behaviors.[2]

Hatfield's lifestyle as a young man looked dramatically different from that of Harold Hughes, his close friend in the Senate. Before Hughes became a committed Christian, he had developed a serious addiction to alcohol and struggled for many years—well into his time in public office—to overcome it. Hatfield never had to make this kind of dramatic change after becoming a serious Christian. Although he spoke about turning his back on his previous Navy lifestyle, he did not suffer as Hughes did from guilt over past behavior.

The changes Hatfield began to make looked more like those made by William Wilberforce a century or so earlier. Both Wilberforce and Hatfield concluded that they should give up some pursuits in order to pursue a life of greater focus and seriousness in following Christ. Both sought a more disciplined lifestyle, fully conscious of the greater political credibility that accompanied a less indulgent set of behaviors. Both also realized their decisions about lifestyle would distance them from some of the social settings in which politicians often developed friendships and support networks. But neither felt that giving up being "one of the boys" hindered their political effectiveness.[3]

Striving for High Ideals

Some of the ethical standards Hatfield applied to his own conduct and to others in public life he drew from the social ideals found broadly in Western culture. He cited, for example, the high ethical standards for public officials articulated by Greek philosophers.

Plato had talked about "philosopher kings," whose authority and effectiveness came partly from their intellect and charisma and partly from their exemplary conduct. Aristotle also contributed substantially to the Western ideas of civic virtue, including the expectation that political leaders should live exemplary lives. Still, Hatfield found these cultural ideals insufficient, since many Greek and Roman leaders failed to live by the ideals they espoused.[4]

Hatfield regretted that the frequent occurrence of corruption and misconduct among public officials produced cynicism and apathy among the citizenry. He appealed to American citizens to join in setting a high standard for officials by acting uprightly themselves and holding officials to account for their actions. He said that the social and political systems that grow the most corrupt reach that point only with the full complicity of the citizens who benefit from official dishonesty.[5]

Hatfield's personal Christian convictions substantially affected his views on political ethics. He realized that some critics—including a few who claimed an adult born-again experience—rejected the idea of a virtuous public official. In fact, he knew that while some in his church felt pleased that he had become much more serious about living the Christian life, they reasoned that if he were a "real" Christian he would opt for a career in the ministry, not in politics. But Hatfield defended the vocation of politics as a legitimate expression of Christian faithfulness, on a par with "full-time Christian service." And he urged Christians not to rule out participation in politics on the grounds that political involvement inevitably corrupts. Without a Christian contribution to public ethics, he argued, public offices would fill up with individuals committed to less than high ideals.[6]

The Danger of Pride

Mark Hatfield enjoyed a rapid and unusually successful pathway into and through state and federal office, subjecting him to one of the classic sins of the Christian faith: pride. Hatfield regularly talked about the temptations of egotism and the resulting pitfalls of wrongdoing when one's position in government made it easy to use political power for personal pleasure or advantage.

More than once Hatfield had pondered the Scripture's account of King David, who had decided that his power entitled him to act upon his lustful thoughts. David's abuse of power started with a distorted sense of his personal worth, leading to a mistaken sense of entitlement and then to harmful indulgence, eventually resulting in both adultery and murder.

Hatfield experienced the precipitous drop from being the most powerful person in the state of Oregon to starting at the very bottom of the U.S. Senate pecking order. It took many years for him to gain extensive power in a system that values seniority over merit. Nevertheless, he experienced many of the perquisites and temptations of his lofty position even from the very beginning. The operators of the trams in the Senate basement always made space for him when he needed to move between buildings. He had a staff that admired and deferred to him, even though he made a point of looking for aides who would challenge his ideas and his positions. He enjoyed a special parking place; he didn't have to worry about getting speeding tickets; and the buttons in the Senate office elevators and in the Capitol allowed him to reverse the car's direction whenever he needed to get to the floor for a vote. Beyond the tangible perks, the halls of powers in the nation's Capitol can have an intoxicating effect.

Hatfield found a potent remedy for egotism and abuse of power in his Christian value system. He often talked about those ideals, exemplified in the teachings and behavior of Jesus. Hatfield called on politicians with ego problems to reflect on Jesus' example of washing others' feet—a task normally reserved for servants and slaves. He invoked Jesus' teaching on servanthood: Christ's followers embarrassed themselves by their backroom maneuvering to gain positions of power, yet Christ instructed them to put aside aspirations for greatness and become like slaves (Luke 22:24-27).

Hatfield said he felt called to use his office to direct public resources to those in greatest need, not to bolster his own power by routing the resources to his friends and supporters. "The purpose of my life," he said, "is to be faithful to Jesus Christ, to follow his way, and to be molded according to the imprint of his life."[7]

The Place of Spiritual Disciplines

It is generally assumed that a life of Christian faith shows itself in frequent prayer, Bible study, and participation in public worship. Hatfield engaged in all these with regularity.

As U.S. senator, Hatfield not only continued to attend church faithfully, but he also went out of his way to speak at various Christian gatherings, especially chapels and assemblies at Christian colleges, universities, and seminaries. Still, one side of Hatfield's piety made him cautious about how he spoke about his faith in public. Many public officials regularly used religious language, but evidenced precious little of the Christian virtues. He often challenged the emptiness of "civil religion" that extolled the ideal of "Christian America." And he took seriously Jesus' admonition to offer one's prayers in private.

Although Hatfield met regularly with other members of the Senate for prayer and Bible study, for example, he generally did not talk publicly about these gatherings. He didn't want anyone to think he claimed a greater piety than his colleagues, so he wanted the prayer sessions off-the-record. One exception was his frequent reference to the Christian fellowship he enjoyed with John Stennis, whose Southern conservatism almost always (ironically) put the two believers on opposite sides of Senate votes.

One finds an even more private expression of Hatfield's Christian faithfulness in his readiness to pray with and counsel members of his staff. The state police officer who served as his driver during his tenure as governor—a fellow Christian—recalled that Hatfield regularly asked him to stop by the roadside so they could pray together. Others on Hatfield's staff would not have called themselves Christians, but nevertheless went to him for understanding and support in times of personal distress. These staff members felt both amazed and moved that their own boss, a United States senator, would drop whatever he was doing to find a quiet place to encourage them and pray for them. Some staff members recall that Hatfield regularly asked them to go with him to pray for colleagues in the Congress or in the executive branch who faced personal crises.[8]

In addition to praying for staff members and colleagues in times of need, Hatfield also gave meaningful help to staff members forced to deal with difficult issues involving their loved ones. One staff member recounted that when his junior-high son suffered a beating, Hatfield handed the staff member the keys to his new car to help him get more quickly to his son's side. This act of kindness left a lasting impression on both the staff member and his son.[9]

The Talking Is Easier Than the Walking

Nothing disillusions citizens more than the discovery that a politician's public statements on moral issues and faith contradict his or her private conduct. It unsettles people when the walk fails to match the talk.

One of Hatfield's long-time peers in the Senate, Robert Packwood, had to resign when several women charged him with abusive and disrespectful behavior—shocking revelations about a senator so well-known for supporting feminist causes. While Hatfield expressed compassion for and respect toward Packwood in this troubling situation, he recognized how Packwood's experiences underscored the need for private behavior to match public image.

Those who served on Hatfield's staff witnessed the consistency of his private conduct with his public morality and Christian ideals.

They describe him as one who respected and valued both those with whom he agreed and those he counted his political enemies. They describe him as one who "walked the talk."[10]

Thorny Issues

Yet a series of events during Hatfield's political career bear examination on this point. One can hardly serve in public office for more than 40 years without *someone* alleging wrongdoing. Journalists have a legitimate duty to investigate the possible wrongdoing of public officials and to inform the public of even the appearance of misconduct. In this vein, critics made a number of allegations about Hatfield's conduct that ultimately did not undermine his reputation and integrity, although they frustrated and even humiliated him.

The first of these allegations came to light during Hatfield's first campaign for governor. The public references to the situation originated not with the press, but with one of Oregon's U.S. senators, Wayne Morse.

In high school Hatfield had been involved in a fatal traffic accident, something no one ever mentioned as he advanced through four levels of elective office in Oregon. He had struck and killed a child and testified that the child had run into the pathway of his car with no warning; he didn't see the child until the moment of impact. While no criminal charges were ever brought, the victim's family prevailed in a subsequent civil action that awarded damages. In the opinion of almost everyone then in public life and in the press, this was a tragic event, but nothing more than an accident.

Morse, however, decided to speak of the accident as an indication of a flaw in Hatfield's character. Even though the two men had been on good terms, Morse asserted that the jury on the case had found Hatfield's testimony inaccurate. In Morse's words, Hatfield had "lied" to the jury; but the judge who heard the case publicly challenged Morse's version of the story.

Although Morse's claims deeply disappointed Hatfield, he went out of his way to avoid returning political fire and subsequently treated Morse as respectfully as he knew how. It is worth noting that no opponent in subsequent campaigns thought it appropriate to bring up the issue.

Two relatively minor controversies arose during Hatfield's first two campaigns for the Senate. In 1966, Don Burden, owner of a group of radio stations including the popular KISN station in Portland, allegedly told his staff to promote Hatfield's candidacy and to speak negatively about his opponent, Congressman Bob Duncan. Meanwhile, Burden contributed to the Hatfield campaign. While the Federal Communications Commission later revoked Burden's license for the KISN station, no one accused the Hatfield campaign of wrongdoing in the case.

In the next Senate campaign in 1972, an oil company contributed to the Republican Senatorial Campaign Committee and asked that the funds be used to assist Hatfield's reelection bid. Critics of such contributions complained that the practice bypassed regulations forbidding political contributions directly from businesses (as opposed to routing the funds through "political action committees"). But statutes in place at the time allowed the practice.[11]

Of far greater consequence was a pair of allegations against Senator Hatfield arising from the real estate career of his wife, Antoinette. At the time of their marriage Antoinette already had a career as an educator, but during the gubernatorial years she concentrated on rearing their children. Along the way Mrs. Hatfield had written cookbooks—not a particularly lucrative way to supplement the family income.

When the Hatfields moved to Washington, Mrs. Hatfield decided to pursue a career in real estate. Expensive Washington homes and a constant turnover of residences gave her the opportunity to do much better financially than she was able to do as a writer. One of her first major transactions involved a purchase by the ambassador of Saudi Arabia. In regard to this sale, the press expressed concern that the buyers might be trying to gain access to the senator by doing business with his wife. Some also pointed to the sale as a measure of Hatfield's supposed "pro-Arab, anti-Israel" mindset. Hatfield pointed out that the latter criticism in particular missed the mark, since Mrs. Hatfield had served as the seller's agent—a seller who happened to be Jewish.

But the more important question was whether Senate spouses ought to be allowed to pursue their own careers without others assuming that their clients wanted to indirectly and inappropriately influence a public official.[12] As two-career political marriages have become more common, Congress has created clearer rules regarding such situations. But at the time, the Hatfields were navigating uncharted waters, something that became even more apparent in another of Mrs. Hatfield's property transactions.

In the early 1980s America had ample reasons to explore alternatives to the nation's reliance on Middle Eastern oil. Fuel shortages in 1973 had resulted in long lines at the gasoline pumps. Then in 1979 the revolution in Iran and the replacement of the shah with the new regime of Ayatollah Khomeini disrupted Iran's oil exports, and a second fuel shortage drove up oil prices around the world. Crude prices peaked at nearly $40 a barrel, a price not reached again until 2006.

Developing new oil supplies in Africa made economic and strategic sense, and exploration and drilling began in Sudan in the mid-1970s. Chevron Oil found commercially viable quantities of oil there in 1981, but Sudan is huge—about the size of western Europe—and its landlocked oil fields could not be developed without a pipeline to move the crude to the country's port on the Red Sea, a distance of some 1,500 kilometers. Seeing an opportunity in the problem, a Greek businessman named Basil Tsakos began soliciting support on Capitol Hill for a pipeline, which he hoped his Trans-Africa Pipeline Corporation could build. The estimated cost at that time was about $10 billion.

As chairman of the Senate Appropriations Committee, Hatfield agreed to talk with Tsakos about the idea and to support it if he felt he could. After their discussion, he wrote to Tsakos endorsing the project; his Senate position made the endorsement significant. But building the pipeline did not need U.S. approval and since this was a private project, federal funding would have been inappropriate. Tsakos merely hoped to establish the idea's credibility in order to attract the kind of investments necessary to go forward.[13]

The Sudan pipeline project later turned out to have merit. It was completed in 1999 with funding from the People's Republic of China, a nation desperate to find new oil sources for its growing economy. But in 1982 Tsakos couldn't attract enough capital to make the project work and he moved on to other things.

The alleged misconduct in this situation centered on a business transaction between Tsakos and Antoinette Hatfield in her role as a Washington realtor. During the period when Tsakos had approached

Hatfield for support, Tsakos employed Mrs. Hatfield to locate an apartment in the prestigious Watergate apartment complex and to oversee its renovation and decoration. It was because Mark and Antoinette Hatfield were husband and wife that the propriety of this business transaction and the amount of Taskos's payments made the news; under other circumstances this certainly would not have received media attention.

The typical "spin" given to this story alleged an excessive fee "obviously intended" to assure Hatfield's support for the pipeline idea. No one declared Hatfield out of line for endorsing the idea of a trans-Sudan pipeline, since it seemed a reasonable idea for reducing the world's reliance on Gulf oil. In fact, no one paid much attention to the situation at all until Jack Anderson, a newspaper columnist with a huge national readership, decided to write about it. Anderson sought to portray Hatfield as less honest than nearly everyone had thought.

In politics, timing is everything. The accusatory stories began to run in mid-1984, during Hatfield's campaign for a fourth term in the Senate. Margie Hendrickson, Hatfield's Democratic opponent, did not miss the political opportunity. She said the Tsakos connection raised serious questions about Hatfield's judgment concerning potential conflicts of interest.[14]

Hatfield had strong feelings that Senate spouses should not be relegated to second-class status, and not be limited to their traditional role of merely attending social functions and rolling bandages during wartime; this perspective complicated Hatfield's response to the allegations. He admired his mother's strong defense of women's equality, and Antoinette strongly embodied similar ideals of female initiative and leadership. Maintaining homes in both Oregon and in the Washington area brought constant financial pressures and he admired Antoinette's business skills. He refused to concede the point that a fee paid to her would inevitably influence his judgment. He and Antoinette often differed on political issues and neither of them expected that he would base his political choices on her preferences. If the stories implied that a Senate spouse could not have her own career, or at least a career in business, then he stood ready to defend her right to contribute to the family income.

Feeling unfairly tried in the Anderson column and in a series of stories in the *New York Times,* Hatfield asked the Senate Ethics Committee to examine the question of a possible connection between Mrs. Hatfield's fee and the senator's support for the pipeline. He asserted that Tsakos would not have been so naïve as to think that Hatfield would go beyond his limited endorsement of the project based on a real estate transaction involving his wife. The immediate political damage decreased when the chair of the Senate Ethics Committee, Ted Stevens of Alaska, announced that he supported the committee staff's findings of insufficient evidence to warrant an investigation.

Meanwhile the Justice Department announced that it would open an investigation into charges that the Tsakos payments amounted to bribes. At one point department investigators concluded that Tsakos probably did intend the fees as payments for access and influence, but more than two years after Hatfield won reelection, the department concluded that any intent by Tsakos to influence Hatfield did not equate to a Hatfield decision to base his action on Tsakos's wishes.[15]

Hatfield ultimately acknowledged his insensitivity to the appearance of a conflict of interest and the couple donated the fees in question to Oregon charities. Still, Hatfield insisted that his wife should not have to answer to the press or to the public about the "reasonableness" of the fees she charged. Oregonians might not expect to pay such large fees for a realtor's services, but most did not understand the economy of a large city such as Washington, D.C. Hatfield continued to defend his wife's integrity, her right to earn a living, and his own integrity in supporting a project on its merits with no thought that his wife's business connections might influence him. But the sting of the charges persisted for many years.[16]

Early in Hatfield's final term in the Senate, investigators and journalists directed a series of charges against him that were potentially more serious than the questions involving Tsakos seven years before. The new charges alleged that Hatfield had received direct and indirect gifts from James Holderman, who had been president of the University of South Carolina. The two had met many years before at an educational conference and continued to see each other regularly after that.

The charges against Hatfield directly involving Holderman included:

- Failure to report the gifts of several art objects from Holderman, said to be worth more than $9,000.

- Failure to report gifts of airline tickets estimated to be worth $5,000.

- Acceptance of a scholarship the Hatfields' son Visko received to attend the University of South Carolina.

The assumption behind each of these allegations was that receiving these items from Holderman might lead to Hatfield's inappropriate support for the university's requests for federal funding, some of which might be handled by the Senate Appropriations Committee.

Journalists and investigators raised the questions about the interaction between Hatfield and Holderman after federal officials indicted Holderman for inappropriately received extra compensation as a university president, and for income-tax evasion. Holderman resigned and pled guilty to some of the charges against him as part of a plea agreement with judicial officials. The allegations against Hatfield asserted that Holderman had been lobbying the Senate Appropriations Committee for an "earmark" appropriation Congress made to the University of South Carolina for an engineering building.[17]

As stories began to appear about these issues, reporters started to write about other matters that seemed to reflect poorly on Hatfield's sensitivity to benefits he or his family might receive from organizations or persons interested in federal legislation:

- The Oregon Health & Science University allegedly used a special admissions policy to admit Hatfield's daughter Elizabeth to their medical school.

- Hatfield had borrowed a substantial sum from his good friend former congressman John Dellenback (Republican from Oregon), who, while employed by an organization of Christian colleges and universities, urged Hatfield to support legislation that would benefit the colleges.[18]

While the Justice Department investigated the allegations, the principal action took place in the Senate Ethics Committee, which took the charges with more seriousness than they had the previous charges involving Basil Tsakos. The committee found that Hatfield's failure to report the various gifts from President Holderman was indeed inappropriate and in violation of Senate rules. While the committee concluded Hatfield had not intentionally failed to report the gifts, they nevertheless issued a strong rebuke. And Hatfield agreed with their conclusion that he had been careless in his reporting. He told the committee, "My mistakes were many and my omissions were serious. There is no one but myself to blame." In an earlier interview he said he regretted that he had had applied his ethical principles to the issues he faced while not sufficiently applying those same principles to the procedural requirements of his office. As part of the committee's action, Hatfield agreed to amend the disclosure forms he had previously submitted to account for the gifts and some forgiven loans. So ended the most difficult and potentially damaging set of charges in Hatfield's public life.[19]

A Serious Follower of Christ

Mark Hatfield never argued that every one of his political actions and statements came without error. He claimed only to be a *serious* follower of Christ, not a *perfect* one. He hoped that his constituents and peers would consider him a person of integrity.

Hatfield gave particular emphasis to the Christian virtues of forgiveness and love. Many times in his career he came to the defense of those condemned for various actions in their roles as public officials, notably Nixon during the Watergate scandal and Oregon senator Packwood for allegations of sexual misconduct.

Hatfield tended to accept and forgive the one who had done wrong, without condoning the wrongdoing. This tendency came both from his sense of personal fallibility and from the Christian teaching to forgive others, since Christians serve a God whose forgiveness knows no limit. It also fit with Hatfield's determination to maintain workable relationships with all those around him, not just with those whose actions he condoned—the subject of the next chapter.

5

RELATIONSHIPS MATTER

Throughout his career, Hatfield took seriously the teachings and example of Jesus about extending love to all people—rich and poor, powerful and weak, evil and godly—and he gave energy and attention to making this spiritual conviction a political principle. He recognized Jesus' emphasis on loving others and noted Jesus' rebuke of his followers who seemed to care more about power and position than about serving others.

As difficult as it could be, Mark Hatfield sought to practice Jesus' teachings about servanthood. And only by understanding that part of his ethical framework can one begin to make sense of some of Hatfield's actions and statements.

A Political Maverick?

Some have inaccurately described Mark Hatfield as a political maverick. Had he in fact felt attracted toward such a pattern, Oregon senator Wayne Morse would have provided an excellent role model.

Morse had represented Oregon in the U.S. Senate for more than two decades by the time Hatfield became the junior senator from Oregon. Throughout his career Morse had functioned as a maverick. His nonconformist streak had motivated him to change parties—twice—settling on the Democratic Party in 1955 after a short stint as an Independent.

According to one of Morse's biographers, Morse's maverick tendencies sprang from his determination to follow his own convictions, to have no master other than his own conscience. Morse would quite willingly sacrifice his political relationships for the sake of his personal commitments. This went beyond political courage, which every successful politician must possess to some degree. By everyone's account, Morse was often argumentative, self-centered, and willing to attack friend or foe.[1]

Hatfield chose not to follow Morse's maverick pathway. Why? For one thing, by personality and inclination Hatfield was an introvert. Casual acquaintances often didn't know or understand his introverted nature, but staff members and other close acquaintances invariably point out that Hatfield was an introvert. Some might associate this part of his personality with the influence of his father, the quieter of his two parents. Many introverts become successful public officials, but they must find ways to function in the midst of the constant pressures of human interaction.

Staff members and friends interacted warmly with Senator Hatfield, but also realized he functioned on a fairly "formal" level with most associates. Virtually no one on the staff called Hatfield by his first name; it was always "Governor" or "Senator." These forms of address indicated respect and a certain distance, though not necessarily a lack of warmth.[2]

Hatfield typically declined invitations to receptions and parties in Washington. Staff members and other associates knew this was another expression of his introverted personality and recognized his preference to spend evenings with his family and his ample collection of books. Intense and uninterrupted interactions with people take an emotional toll on introverts and Hatfield became weary of the endless parade of individuals who wanted to see him and to present their political issues and requests.

Because of his personal tendencies and the pedestal on which public officials tend to get placed, Hatfield had to make a determined effort to develop and nurture relationships at various levels. In his book *Between a Rock and a Hard Place,* he spoke of the enormous obstacles in the congressional culture to developing and sustaining healthy relationships. He spoke of the almost worshipful ways members of Congress are treated. Once, for example, he stepped off a plane and into a hectic schedule of meetings and press conferences. His hosts hadn't grasped that he would need a restroom break and he had a difficult time persuading them that they really could stop at the nearest service station to allow him to take care of his personal needs. Later, to communicate this point to a new staff member, Hatfield paused outside a men's room and jokingly insisted that the staff member not overlook the needs of the body while helping to organize schedules.[3]

Hatfield understood that the almost worshipful respect given him by constituents and staff members in the Capitol complex hindered the formation of healthy relationships. Such treatment often leads to egotism, a professional hazard that makes sustaining warm relationships difficult.[4] In his political memoir *Against the Grain,* Hatfield devoted an entire chapter to relationships, citing some the hindrances to his own relationship because of political differences and troublesome experiences. He began the chapter with a statement he made many times: "Politics is fundamentally an exercise in human relations. And it's an exercise which takes skill, strength, patience, and truckloads of hard, constant work."

As Hatfield reflected on the political career behind him, he declared that it had always been his goal to build lasting friendships with his peers, based on compassion and respect. He maintained that a healthy political relationship could survive strong difference of opinion, a lofty goal for an office holder. In this chapter we will examine his efforts to achieve this ideal with respect to his peers, his subordinates, and his constituents.[5]

Relationships with Peers

Hatfield's relationships with a sampling of his peers illustrate both the successes and the near failures of his trying to implement his ideals.

Wayne Morse

As already noted, Hatfield had a challenging relationship with Senator Wayne Morse. Hatfield's first difficult interaction with Morse occurred after both won election as delegates to the Republican National Convention. Hatfield seemed a logical choice for delegate, since he headed up Eisenhower's Oregon campaign committee and everyone expected the convention to nominate Eisenhower for president. Meanwhile, Morse intended to play a prominent role in the convention as Oregon's senior senator.

But when Oregon's caucus of delegates passed over Morse in favor of Hatfield for the convention's prestigious platform committee, ill feelings ensued. Oregon's Republican governor, Douglas McKay, had helped orchestrate this outcome in response to Morse's shaky loyalty to the Republican Party. Morse didn't directly blame Hatfield for the decision, but the situation definitely irked him. Hatfield tried to deflect Morse's anger by regularly briefing the senator on committee discussions and by seeking his counsel regarding its decisions, but the seeds of ill will had been planted.[6]

Six years later, during Hatfield's first race for governor, Morse publicly attacked Hatfield for his involvement in a fatal accident *(see chapter 4)*. Few, if any, public officials agreed with Morse's tactic and it ended up injuring Morse's reputation more than it hurt Hatfield's gubernatorial chances. Hatfield later characterized Morse's statements as the "worst smear tactics possible," but at the time he refrained from public statements against Morse.[7]

Hatfield credits a mutual friend, Glenn Jackson, with helping to restore the relationship with Morse. Jackson, a prominent business leader from southern Oregon, had a history of public service, including service as chair of the Oregon Highway Commission. Both men highly respected Jackson, as did most other state leaders. In a meeting Jackson arranged, Morse talked on and on about the rare breed of cattle he owned, called Devons—a topic he frequently discussed whether anyone seemed interested or not. Neither man said anything about their political differences; instead Hatfield allowed the conversation to center on Morse's cattle, and the meeting accomplished its purpose. Both Morse and Hatfield subsequently functioned as allies rather than enemies during Hatfield's remaining years as governor. Moreover, Morse supported Hatfield in his first Senate race against Congressman Bob Duncan.[8]

Morse introduced his new junior colleague to the Senate in January 1967, per custom, and did it with a gracious spirit that reflected their restored relationship. But then in 1972 Morse filed as Hatfield's opponent since Morse had no desire to retire from Congress after Bob Packwood defeated him in 1968. Given Morse's outspoken history, this could have become a difficult situation, but Hatfield soon realized Morse had done him a favor. At the time Hatfield seemed very vulnerable on his stance toward the Vietnam War, just as he had been in 1966. Having a general election opponent who opposed the war just as adamantly as Hatfield himself turned out to be a political blessing. Both candidates presented their strengths and positions in the campaign and refrained from attacking one another. Even though Morse did criticize Hatfield for being too loyal to President Nixon, it was a dubious criticism, and it strengthened Hatfield's standing with loyal Republicans, especially with those who had wondered about his support for the party.[9]

A fitting conclusion to the Morse-Hatfield relationship occurred with Morse's death in 1974. Until the moment he passed away, Morse continued to work to regain his seat in the Senate. After his death, the Morse family invited Hatfield to deliver the eulogy in the National Cathedral in Washington and at the Oregon State capitol in Salem. Some advisers counseled Hatfield not to speak at the memorial services, but he declared it to be a great honor and had no thought of dwelling on the difficulties of the past. Moreover, Hatfield genuinely admired the intellect and passion Morse brought to his political career, once speaking of Morse's "sheer, absolute brilliance."[10]

Tom McCall

Significant frictions also developed from time to time between Hatfield and other Republican office holders in Oregon. So painful were the memories of his clashes with the man who succeeded him as Oregon's governor, Tom McCall, that Hatfield debated whether to discuss the issue in his published memoirs. He finally decided to talk about it as an example of the importance of personal relationships in politics and to acknowledge that he might have done more to address the differences that arose between the two gifted leaders.

At times the friction resulted from the fact that the two men held similar views and aspirations as progressive Republicans and competed with one another for support. Other problems arose from their dissimilar personalities. McCall was outspoken, mercurial, and assertive, in some ways like Wayne Morse. His wide experience in journalism made him an expert at cultivating the trust of the media. Hatfield was more reserved and not so likely to appear to be everyone's "buddy." He often felt uncomfortable in dealing with the press.

When Hatfield won his first campaign for governor in 1958, he had to appoint someone to succeed himself as secretary of state for the remaining two years of his term. McCall thought Hatfield had promised or implied that McCall would get the position, but Hatfield insisted he hadn't made such a commitment and appointed Howell Appling instead. McCall ultimately won election to the post, but not until six years later—an unwelcome delay for which McCall blamed Hatfield.

The conflict reached greater intensity in 1971 when Hatfield prepared to run for reelection to the Senate. Governor McCall publicly stated that he might run against Hatfield in the Republican primary, citing the Vietnam War as the principal reason. McCall emphatically supported Nixon's war policies and the governor told the press he felt his son in the Navy deserved more support from state officials than what Hatfield was giving.[11]

To their credit, McCall and Hatfield talked privately about the possibility of McCall's run for the Senate; both knew it could hurt either or both of their political careers. The conversation apparently did not go well, however, and ended with Hatfield inviting McCall to run against him and assuring him it would be a tough battle. McCall ultimately backed away from filing for the office after speaking with President Nixon. Nixon might have preferred to have someone more supportive than Hatfield in the Senate, but he knew a lot of political blood would get spilled in a Hatfield-McCall primary race. Nixon also knew a Hatfield-McCall primary battle might make it difficult for the Republican victor to defeat the Democratic opponent in the fall—and he feared such an outcome might hurt his own chances of reelection in 1972. Different advice from Nixon might well have tipped the balance toward a McCall candidacy.[12]

Bob Packwood

Hatfield's relationship with his Senate colleague, Bob Packwood, involved some other significant challenges. As a student at Willamette, Packwood had enrolled in several political science classes taught by Professor Hatfield. In some ways he benefited from Hatfield's demonstration that a progressive Republican could succeed in Oregon, despite the dominance of conservatives in the GOP. Since both men were moderate Republicans, however, they inevitably competed for public attention. And at times grass-roots party volunteers had to choose which of the two senators they would most actively support.

Like Governor McCall, Packwood felt comfortable in relating to reporters and had a good sense of what seemed newsworthy. For years Hatfield made a point of not having a staff member assigned primarily to press relations and gave only limited attention to cultivating media goodwill. By contrast, Packwood's aides went out of their way to make sure their boss scored the most "points" with the press and with Oregon's citizens when it came time to announce newly approved federal programs.

Other irritants between the two political leaders complicated the relationship. The first involved Hatfield's 1968 support for Wayne Morse and other senators who opposed the Vietnam War. Hatfield did not single out Morse for his endorsement, but Packwood took offense that his former professor would express general support for the Democratic incumbent. Morse had helped lead the opposition to U.S. involvement in Vietnam, so Hatfield would have found it awkward to overlook him in expressing support for antiwar senatorial candidates.

In hindsight, Hatfield might have helped the situation by privately explaining to Packwood that he needed to acknowledge Morse's stand on Vietnam, while in other ways he would try to support Packwood. Since Hatfield failed to do this, their relationship suffered—and it didn't improve after Packwood won the race.[13]

The Packwood-Hatfield relationship got an even more severe test in 1972, the year McCall and Hatfield locked horns over McCall's possible candidacy. Rumors swirled in Oregon that Packwood had encouraged McCall to run. The rumor-mongers reasoned that a McCall victory would result in Packwood becoming the senior Oregon senator, which in turn meant he could choose to serve on the Senate committees on which Hatfield had served. The rumors were an irritation, even though they were never confirmed or denied.[14]

Packwood and Hatfield regularly disagreed on foreign affairs and military policy. Hatfield passed up few opportunities to challenge new military expenditures, especially for what he considered redundant military hardware, and he had spent the first part of his Senate career challenging both Democratic and Republic presidents about American involvement in Vietnam. Commonly labeled a "hawk," Packwood had a stance on defense and foreign affairs more typical of his party.

The Supreme Court decision on abortion—handed down in the first year of Hatfield's second term and during the middle of Packwood's first term—divided the two senators even more sharply. The two men took opposite positions on abortion and remained on opposite sides of the issue throughout their overlapping time in the Senate. Packwood supported the court's decision that women should have the right to choose abortions; over time he became one of the greatest supporters of pro-choice and women's rights groups in Congress. Hatfield, on the other hand, based his pro-life position on what he characterized as a consistent pro-life position, critical not only of abortion, but also of unnecessary wars, of euthanasia, and of capital punishment *(see chapter 12)*. Hatfield never became emphatic and zealous enough in his opposition to abortion to suit the more strident pro-life groups, but he generally got their endorsement, something that Packwood never sought or experienced.

Hatfield and Packwood approached congressional politics quite differently. Packwood, a lawyer, participated in political debate as a zealous proponent or opponent of a particular position. His training shaped this way of thinking, and like the skillful debater he was, he could argue either side effectively. As a result, it was sometimes difficult to see a clear pattern in the positions he took. As a pragmatist, he felt at liberty to choose where to stand, depending on the alignment of forces on a question and the political gains that might accrue from taking a particular position. Hatfield focused more directly on the principles underlying an issue and had less interest in the political maneuvering.

These numerous differences between the two senators make it remarkable that their relationship remained as positive as it did. When each gained the chairmanship of important Senate committees—Packwood over finance and Hatfield over appropriations—they knew how much their cooperation would benefit Oregon projects, so most of the time they worked effectively together. As Hatfield later recalled, "[Packwood] can strategize issues better than anyone I know and had no peer in the Senate when it came to dissecting, analyzing, or debating certain issues, especially regarding taxes."[15]

Senator Packwood played a significant and constructive part in one of Hatfield's most contentious clashes with party leadership in the Senate, near the end of his final term in office. Hatfield had decided to oppose a "balanced budget" measure on the grounds that it would create nothing more than the appearance of curtailing federal spending while doing little to balance the coming year's budget. He also argued that overriding provisions of the Constitution with a three-fifths vote of the Congress would set a dangerous precedent. Hatfield displayed the same fear he had expressed in the Senate many other times: that budget-balancing would mean cutting programs for the poor and needy, while defense spending would remain untouched. He had treated other budget balancing proposals with similar skepticism, despite his fiscally conservative values.[16]

As Republican leaders in the Senate began to count votes, they realized they needed Hatfield's support, and so they began to pressure their Oregon colleague to fall in line. Despite their differences on many issues, Hatfield's relationship with fellow Republicans Orrin Hatch of Utah and Robert Dole had been uniformly warm. As the floor leader for the balanced-budget measure, Hatch tried everything he could think of to get Hatfield's backing, including having Robert Schuler, pastor of the Crystal Cathedral in California, come to speak with him. As the vote approached, Senator Dole literally begged his colleague either to change his mind or "take a hike" during the vote. Hatfield said he wouldn't do either, but would resign from the Senate if the vote seemed that important to Dole.

Hatfield's "no" vote did indeed prevent the measure's passage, provoking some angry Republicans to propose that the Senate caucus force Hatfield to resign from his position as chair of the Appropriations Committee. But Packwood helped put an end to this revenge move against Hatfield, warning his colleagues that forcing a senior party member out of his chairmanship would amount to political cannibalism.[17]

Packwood's reluctant resignation from the Senate in 1995 reveals one further measure of the durability of the Hatfield-Packwood relationship. The resignation came after Packwood tried unsuccessfully to defend himself against charges of sexual misconduct, accusations made by numerous women. Additionally he stood accused of interfering with the investigation.

Although Hatfield understood the necessity of Packwood's resignation, he took no joy in his colleague's departure. A few years later, after his own retirement from the Senate, Hatfield expressed in his memoirs the sadness he felt for the women hurt by Packwood's conduct; for his colleague's wife and family members so profoundly injured by the situation; and for the loss to the Senate of one of its most effective members, whom he called a "brilliant politician."[18]

Relationships with Subordinates

Those who serve in high national offices tend to have few peers and many subordinates. Hatfield's early political career in Oregon showed the opposite tendency.

Oregon had a "citizen legislature," with biennial sessions that lasted only part of every other year. The legislature had only enough in its budget to hire one staff member per elected official, with their "offices" located in the House and Senate chamber, where the member and his or her secretary sat side by side. When Hatfield won election to the full-time position of secretary of state in 1957, he at last had the opportunity to hire several staff members. At that point he began a process of forming many long-term and close relationships with his staff members, wherever he served.

Gubernatorial Staff

One of the earliest and strongest of those relationships was with Travis Cross. Hatfield had casually known Cross while both grew up in Salem. He had attended the First Baptist Church with Cross and developed a close friendship with him while both studied at Stanford University. Cross became Hatfield's political confidant and strategist when they returned to Oregon and both accepted positions at their alma mater, Willamette University. Cross continued as Hatfield's volunteer political consultant, helping with legislative races, finally joining his gubernatorial staff as press secretary.

Shortly after Hatfield became governor, Warne Nunn joined his staff. Nunn graduated from Willamette a few years before Hatfield and had headed up the state's Motor Vehicles Division. To this staff were added Leolyn Barnett, secretary; and Loren Hicks, legal counsel. The members of this group developed lasting and close personal friendships with each other; in fact, Hicks took time from his retirement to serve as treasurer in the last Hatfield campaign.[19]

Senate Staff

After Hatfield's election to the Senate, most of his Oregon staff members chose not to accompany him to Washington. So he set about to assemble a staff made up of some Oregonians and others who applied for positions because of their support for his foreign policy positions, his Christian principles, or both.

As Hatfield stepped into the Capitol Hill culture, it bothered him that so many staff members seemed to blindly support "the boss." As governor he had counted on his staff to help him understand positions different from his own and even to argue with him about his views. So as he hired staff members in Washington (with the help of his long-time staff director Sam Mallicoat, and later Gerry Frank), he looked for talented women and men who were thoughtful and articulate, and who expressed a serious interest in public-policy issues. Above all, he wanted individuals courageous enough to disagree with him.

One might have predicted that Hatfield's staff members would share his Christian faith and his loyalty to the Republican Party, but such was not always the case. The interview and hiring process typically took place without any apparent effort to determine their party or their faith. Some key members of the staff were Jewish; Hatfield affirmed them in their faith and welcomed their comments about his policies on Israel. Some staff members joked about Christians and "lions" on his staff, a reference both to those who fully shared Hatfield's evangelical Christian experience and to those who did not. Everyone understood that lions would not draft his notes for speeches and sermons to be given to Christian audiences, but the non-Christian staff experienced few if any obstacles in functioning effectively. Many staff members aligned more with the Democratic Party than with the Republicans—and such political diversity suited Hatfield.

A close convergence of ideology and spirituality encouraged Hatfield to form a special bond with a few on his staff, including Wes Michaelson *(see chapter 2)*. In a number of cases, he spent time with staff members helping them cope with personal and family struggles. He expressed support for them and offered to pray with them.

Hatfield often functioned more like a professor than a boss in his relationships with staff members and interns. He went out of his way to make internships a meaningful learning experience for college students who earned credit for their work in Washington. He took them on special tours of the Capitol and made a point of interacting with them whenever possible. Staff meetings sometimes resembled seminars more than strategy sessions. One staff member recalls Hatfield going around the room at one meeting and asking each staff member what books they were reading.[20]

Another side of Hatfield's relationships with staff members came out in the privacy of the office when he passed along jokes politely described as "irreverent." Sometimes he would offer not-so-flattering imitations of prominent figures in Congress or the White House. Once he rode down the hall of the Senate office building on a tricycle that someone had donated to needy children. As staff members became aware of Hatfield's unusual sense of humor, they recognized a personality more complex than indicated by his reputation as a dignified, formal, and even aloof individual. He definitely had a "senatorial" bearing, but his staff found him both warm and approachable.

Staff members came to realize they had considerable access to Hatfield, so long as they didn't overdo this privilege. One of his boundaries with staff members reflected his personality. He welcomed dialogue with staff members about particular issues and desired to hear from them when they felt troubled about positions he had taken. But he didn't generally make decisions about his stand on new issues on the basis of staff recommendations alone. He welcomed the information and arguments staff presented and then processed the decision on his own. So long as staff members respected his method of decision making, they were able to exercise considerable influence over his ideas and positions.[21]

An introvert, Hatfield felt uncomfortable expressing difficult concerns to a staff member about his or her performance, much less terminating someone's employment. So he made sure he had a staff director who could do this, and for most of the Senate years this responsibility fell to Gerry Frank. Frank had an extensive background in business and knew how to "crack the whip" in a firm but fair way.

The expectations placed on staff members to be diligent and productive did not stand in the way of their developing close, long-lasting friendships with each other and with Senator Hatfield.

Capitol Hill Employees

Those who spent time with Senator Hatfield noticed that he made a point of developing acquaintances and even friendships with various Senate employees outside his own staff. For example, he came to know many workers responsible for protecting and assisting the members of Congress. Police officers were on hand to protect members of Congress from embittered terrorists and deranged constituents. Elevator operators knew how to show respect and courtesy to members of the Senate to allow them to get to the Senate chambers or committee rooms quickly. Tram operators did their part to make sure members had priority in moving between the buildings. Cooks and servers prepared and served meals in the many restaurants on Capitol Hill, some for members only.

Hatfield recognized the social distance between most members and the service employees, and he tried hard to span this distance by learning the employees' names and inquiring regularly about their well-being and about their families. When he noticed these workers were dealing with problems, he would encourage them and ask how he could help. In all these expressions of interest he was trying to step outside the elite-servant model, which condoned the treatment of Senate employees as nameless and unimportant.

In this regard Hatfield found a kindred spirit in his former pastor, Richard Halverson, who became Senate chaplain in 1981. Both Hatfield and Halverson reached out to the Capitol employees as friends and peers, ready to listen and pray together when they expressed special needs.[22]

Relationships with Constituents

Politicians succeed only when they attend to the needs and concerns of their constituents. Elected officials who ignore this truism rarely serve more than one term in office. From the early days of his political career, Hatfield understood that his success depended on regularly and systematically visiting his constituents and responding to their needs. He knew that his interaction with his constituents must include more than giving speeches and shaking hands during his visits around the state. It required meaningful discussions with them both in Oregon and in the nation's capital, seeking to understand the basis for the opinions they expressed. It also required that he be attentive to every-one in the state, not just the opinion leaders and those with political clout.

But as we have noted, it appeared by the end of Hatfield's first term in the Senate that his effectiveness in building close relationships with his constituents had not been working as well as it had during his years as an officeholder in Oregon. His close friend and political advisor, Gerry Frank, had heard from Oregonians the same thing that Hatfield had heard—that Hatfield had not been communicating with the voters as effectively as he intended. Frank worked actively with the 1972 campaign to overcome this problem; then after the campaign Frank agreed to go to Washington as administrative assistant, the Senate's understated job title for chief of staff.

Taking on something of a "good cop, bad cop" partnership with the senator, Frank laid down the law that staff members respond promptly (at the latest, within 48 hours) to letters and phone calls from Oregon. No matter how important they felt their other work might be, constituent communication had to come first. Tom Imeson, who became one of Hatfield's most effective staff members in a number of roles, recalls an unpleasant experience with the "48-hour rule" when he was a junior member of the staff. Frank discovered that Imeson had apparently been slow in responding to some constituents, and he had a "woodshed" session with Imeson about the issue. Imeson felt embarrassed and frustrated—so much so that he later said he was going to resign. Frank declined to accept the resignation, but insisted that the infraction not happen again.[23]

Frank also began orchestrating more frequent and systematic trips for the senator to Oregon, drawing on the information in a remarkable set of records he had put together about key persons in every community in Oregon. The records, mostly on 3" by 5" cards, provided an amazing resource on people in leadership and those who had contacted Senator Hatfield in the past, along with those people's birthdays and anniversaries. The cards were the place to find people who could organize Hatfield's community visits. They also allowed Frank to remember those whom he and the Senator would encounter during the community visits. By everyone's account, Hatfield had an exceptional memory for people he encountered along the way. Sometimes the cards had prompted the memory and sometimes he was able to recall names and personal details with no assistance at all.[24]

One of Hatfield's more unusual but favorite ways of relating to his constituents was to break away from his busy schedule to take visitors from Oregon to see the interesting and little-known features of the Capitol building. He had served as a tour guide in the Oregon capitol building as a college student, and delighted in being able to take people to places not on the typical tour of the U.S. Capitol, such as the restored room in which the Supreme Court once met. After he became chair of the Senate Appropriations Committee, he helped see that funds were provided to restore a number of other historically important areas in the building.

A Commitment to Love Others

The warm friendships that Hatfield formed with peers, with subordinates, and with constituents were all a part of his effort to be faithful to one of the most basic of Christ's teachings: to love others. When political differences arose, he did his best to focus on the issues and not attack the people. When it was common for others in Congress to keep a close accounting of who were friends and who were enemies, Hatfield tried to treat even his opponents as valued partners in crafting public policy.

And in relating to staff members and the people who filled the servant roles for Congress, Hatfield tried to honor the "love one another" teachings of Jesus. This principle of loving one's "enemies"— not just one's friends—was in turn the basis for Hatfield's consistent advocacy for peace and justice, the subject of our next chapter.

6

SEEKING PEACE AND JUSTICE

No issue created more uneasiness among Hatfield's conservative constituents than his position on war and peace. And no issue so clearly places him on the progressive side of the political scale among evangelicals. In later discussions on the Vietnam War *(see chapters 8 and 9)*, we will see that Hatfield's position on that conflict shaped his entry into national politics and nearly sidetracked his election to Congress. As it turned out, his stance gave him some brief national notoriety as one of a handful of congressional leaders determined to get the United States out of Vietnam as quickly as possible.

Not Easy to Label

Like many aspects of Hatfield's political life, his positions on war and peace are not easy to label and categorize. Many Mennonite pacifists lived in Dallas, Oregon, where he grew up, but Hatfield never became a pacifist in the sense of refusing to participate in military service.[1] Mark Hatfield's "conversion" to peace came not from his Mennonite neighbors in Oregon, but in such unlikely places as Iwo Jima, Okinawa, Hiroshima, and Vietnam. His combat experiences deeply impacted his worldview and transformed him into a zealot for peace, as we will explore.

Few national leaders in the second half of the twentieth century worked as diligently and consistently as Hatfield in their efforts for peace. But Hatfield didn't fit into the conscientious-objector category, even though his foes often attacked him as an unpatriotic pacifist. Nor could he be wedged into the much larger theological view we call the "just-war" perspective (based on Augustine's criteria for endorsing and participating in military actions). One must seek a different label for Mark Hatfield—or better yet, throw out the labels altogether and identify him as one who saw no paradox in being both pacifist and patriot.

Hatfield questioned U.S. participation in many 20th-century wars, most especially the one in Vietnam, but he did not believe a free world could continue to exist without sometimes engaging in military actions. Nevertheless, when he enrolled in college in 1940, he was not one of those eager for the United States to enter World War II. He described his international values at that time as isolationist; the first global war in which his father had served had persuaded him and his family that the struggles of the Europeans should be left to them to settle. But on December 7, 1941, the world radically changed for Mark Hatfield, as it did for many other isolationists.

The Japanese attack on Pearl Harbor that day was enough to convince Hatfield and many others that *this* war was both essential and right—and that he must do his part in it. A college student at the time, he joined a local Naval Reserve unit as he continued through the remainder of his undergraduate work, preparing to accept a commission as an officer in the Navy. Shortly after enlisting, Hatfield got his training on naval bases in New York and California, and then received his orders for combat duty on Iwo Jima.

The Iwo Jima memorial in Washington, like many others, honors the heroism of American soldiers. It features U.S. Marines who at great loss of life secured American control over the small Pacific island of Iwo Jima in early 1945. Some 70,000 Marines participated in the bloody attack.

As commander of a group of ten landing craft, Hatfield had orders to deliver Marines to the beach so the corps could gain control over the island. The airfields and harbors of Iwo Jima held great strategic importance for the Allies, since this island remained one of the last major Japanese strongholds outside of Japan itself. Taking the island would curtail Japanese air attacks in other locations and would provide a departure point for U.S. bombers headed for the Japanese mainland.

The bloody climax of the battle in February and March 1945 made it clear the Japanese stood ready to suffer extreme losses to hold the island. Despite more than two months of American bombing, the Japanese hold on the small island remained strong. Hiding in tunnels on Mt. Surabachi, defending troops were positioned and equipped to direct lethal fire on the Marines as the Marines landed. By battle's end the United States had lost nearly 7,000 troops, while the Japanese suffered more than triple those losses.

While no Japanese artillery fire hit Hatfield or his unit during the Iwo Jima landing operations, he spoke later of the horror of the experience. He described the deafening noise of guns and bombs of all descriptions and the mangled bodies he and his men took back to the ship. The carnage very much resembled scenes depicted in films such as *Flags of our Fathers* and *Saving Private Ryan* that came out many years later. Hatfield never enjoyed watching such films, for his memories of the real battle remained so horrible. Eventually, the landing crafts' mother ship had to transport the wounded to a hospital in Saipan, thus ending Hatfield's involvement in the battle.[2]

Hatfield's next wartime experience, in Okinawa, felt less intense than that in Iwo Jima, though the Japanese continued to defend that island just as stubbornly. By the time Hatfield's unit got to Okinawa, the Marines had put down much of the island's resistance, but serious dangers still lurked in the area. Kamikaze pilots and Japanese swimmers loaded themselves with explosives and targeted American ships, like the one that carried Hatfield. One plane headed directly toward Hatfield's ship, but at the last moment veered off and destroyed a nearby ship instead.[3]

The final mission planned for Hatfield's unit would have delivered the Americans to a far more horrific battlefield. In preparation for the invasion of Japan itself, the American fleet conducted training exercises in the Philippines. But when U.S. pilots dropped an atomic bomb on Hiroshima and an even more powerful bomb on Nagasaki, the Japanese surrendered, thus ending any need for an invasion. So Hatfield's ship instead proceeded to Japan to prepare for an American occupation.

Navy commanders selected Hatfield and other officers to visit Hiroshima to inspect the damage done by the first nuclear bomb. The bomb had detonated just a month earlier and walking around the devastated city overwhelmed Lieutenant Hatfield. Later he spoke of his shock at the ruined buildings, the stench of dead bodies, and the utter desolation of the landscape. He watched with sadness as survivors wandered among the ruins, looking for any trace of family and friends and hoping to find a few scattered possessions. He shuddered to think what the world might be like if nuclear bombs became the ultimate weapon of choice in future global conflicts.[4]

Encounters in Hiroshima with the civilian victims of war touched Hatfield even more than did the general devastation he witnessed. Although these men and women had survived the bomb, they didn't know if they could survive the loss of everything they needed to stay alive *after* the bomb. Hatfield's group did not visit areas where badly burned victims barely clung to life, but nearly everyone they saw appeared terrified, intimidated, and hungry. The Navy men knew they couldn't do much about the terror, but they began giving children their lunches to help in a small way with the hunger. Here they had come face-to-face with the "enemy"—an enemy now completely helpless—and they could no longer view the people as enemies.

Hatfield picked up a small child one day, and pity and affection replaced the hatred that he and many Americans had felt for the Japanese since the attack on Pearl Harbor. He said:

> Here were people I dehumanized in my mind throughout the war, thinking of them as one vast, massive enemy, not human, not like any of us. Now on their shore I knew the brilliant truth. They were exactly like us, suffering, afraid—human. Oh, so human. As the adults relaxed and smiled, as my lunch was completely given to the children, my loathing vanished. I stood awash, clean in an epiphany which has never deserted me. Hatred had gushed out, transmuted into the powerful balm of compassion.[5]

The lessons of Japan went far beyond the horror of nuclear weapons; that part was obvious. The more profound lessons concerned the horrible truth that human beings—doing what they saw as necessary and right—had decided to turn thousands of innocent civilians into charred bodies. Many times this global conflict had seen widespread destruction of civilian lives, especially in Europe, but Hiroshima had suffered this devastation on a totally different scale.

Hatfield returned to his ship a changed person, one who could never again think like those of the "realist" school; he simply could not conceive of war as a normal and natural way to pursue foreign policy. While other veterans might speak of heroism, danger, and camaraderie—things Hatfield knew well—Hatfield chose instead to talk about the visceral shock of seeing the walking dead of Hiroshima.

Not Quite a Pacifist

As profoundly as Hatfield's World War II experience had moved him, and as intense as his later opposition to the Vietnam War became, he never took up the pacifism of his childhood neighbors in Dallas, Oregon. In his memoir, published after the end of his political career, he declared he was not and never had been a pacifist, for he did not oppose the use of all military force in a conflict such as World War II.[6]

One could be excused for missing this point, particularly since Hatfield's opposition to the Vietnam War became so strong that he came close to putting himself in the category of "selective conscientious objection." In fact, the Vietnam conflict produced many newly convinced pacifists who had no connection to one of the historically pacifist religious movements, such as the Mennonites. These individuals couldn't say they would always refuse induction into the military, but they insisted they could never serve in a war like Vietnam.

In *Between a Rock and a Hard Place,* Hatfield ponders what he might have done had he been born a generation later and the government had drafted him to serve in Vietnam. To take part in that conflict would have violated both his conscience and his faith, he said. Based on his gut-wrenching experiences in World War II, his 1945 visit to Indochina, and his observation of later events in the area, he concluded that he would have chosen to become a selective conscientious objector.[7]

The combination of Hatfield's visits to Hiroshima and Vietnam sowed seeds that came close to germinating into complete pacifism. Close—but not quite all the way.

Defending the "Purist" Model

Some later described Hatfield as a "peace senator," meaning he seemed to oppose all wars, and believed war had become an unacceptable tool of foreign policy. This is inaccurate.

Hatfield, in *Between a Rock and a Hard Place,* called such a stand for national nonviolence the "purist" model. He said a purist would refuse to participate in any violence, and particularly would not agree to military service. He said such a person would also refuse to serve in law enforcement, because such a career might require the taking of human life. A purist also could never become president of the

United States, because that role requires serving as commander in chief of the armed forces.

Hatfield said the purist extends his or her pacifist convictions from the personal level to the national-policy arena. The purist stands in opposition to *any* use of force by a nation against other nations. "Peace cannot be built through terror, through threats of mutual retaliation, and through war," said Hatfield in summarizing the purist position.[8]

Although he did not support the purist model, Hatfield disagreed with those who characterized it as a withdrawal from the evils of the political world. He praised Mahatma Gandhi as a prime example of a purist who fully engaged the colonial political system and its many injustices. Gandhi remained committed to seeking justice with a combination of persuasion and pressure, mobilizing the people to immobilize the tyrants.

Hatfield also cited Harvard scholar Gene Sharp as a contemporary example of an engaged purist. In his research, Sharp discovered many examples of nonviolent citizen resistance to political oppression. Taking his cue from Sharp's work, Hatfield acknowledged that national nonviolent resistance does not always "succeed" in the sense of solving problems or preventing the loss of life. But the way of the purist, he said, holds as much or more promise for success as the way of the warrior.[9]

Long after the Vietnam War, Senator Hatfield continued to respect the conscientious objection position that he himself could not fully embrace. One form of this conviction is called "war-tax resistance." Some conscientious objectors have reasoned that they must refuse to pay the portion of their income taxes used for national defense—both present expenditures and interest on the national debt incurred from past wars and veterans benefits. During many sessions of Congress, Hatfield cosponsored legislation to allow those who would qualify as conscientious objectors to divert their war taxes to human service programs. This legislation was a response to some war-tax resisters who notified the Internal Revenue Service that they were donating to human-service agencies the money they would have paid as war taxes. The war tax bill never received serious consideration by tax committees in Congress, and those who withheld taxes had these amounts garnished from their bank accounts or paychecks. But for

Hatfield to support such legislation as a non-pacifist seemed remarkable.

Clarifying the Apologist Model

Hatfield used the term *apologist* to describe the other end of the war-and-peace continuum. The apologist understands and accepts the validity of personal pacifism, Hatfield says, but will not extend those convictions to the nation.

The individual can practice the ethics of self-giving love, even to the point of accepting personal harm or martyrdom, but national leaders committed to the preservation of their society cannot rule out the use of violence. The very existence of the government may be at stake, as well as the just treatment of its citizens.

Hatfield's analysis of the apologist model looks very similar to the just-war position, introduced by Saint Augustine in the fourth century and accepted by most Christians ever since. But Hatfield applied an important clarification of the just-war view: Augustine never meant his just-war theory to justify *every* opportunity for war that might come along, Hatfield insisted. In particular, it should not be used to provide a theological grounding for the realist school of foreign policy. He intended his position to condone only truly just wars—those that held up under the rigorous scrutiny.

Most, if not all wars in U.S. history had been justified on the basis of the just-war position, even though few of those wars actually met Augustine's criteria. This bothered Hatfield. Even some aspects of combat in World War II could be called into question, he said, because of the use of bombing campaigns that wiped out entire civilian populations. And the U.S. refusal to rule out the first use of nuclear weapons in later years completely violated just-war criteria, he asserted.[10]

Choosing a Middle Way

After examining both the purist and apologist positions, Hatfield concluded he could not fully embrace either. He said he could not completely endorse the just-war position, nor was he a pacifist in either the personal or the national sense.

Is it possible to identify a position that aligns well with Hatfield's views on war and peace? Scholars in the peace studies field have looked for a suitable label for a position that takes something of a middle way between just war and pacifism. *Peacekeeping* is too narrow, since it typically refers to the work of United Nations troops enforcing ceasefire agreements and curtailing violence while further negotiations occur. *Peacemaking* is also an overly narrow term, since it primarily refers to the activities of public officials and diplomats who negotiate acceptable peace agreements. Notre Dame University professor John Paul Lederach and other peace-studies scholars favor the term *peacebuilding*, since it embraces so many of the long-range efforts toward both "negative peace" (stopping the violence) and "positive peace" (building an infrastructure for long-range reconciliation and rebuilding).[11]

Lederach's definition of peacebuilding seems to fit well with the breadth of convictions that Senator Hatfield espoused—convictions that reached far beyond the question of personal and national engagement in war. Consider a few of the positions that characterized Mark Hatfield as a peacebuilder:

Opposing the Vietnam War — A political pragmatist would not have taken a position on the Vietnam War in the way Hatfield did or at the time he did. Twice he stood alone in opposition to pro-Vietnam War resolutions at national governors' conferences. The second time he had begun his first campaign for the Senate, knowing that the overwhelming majority of Oregonians supported the war.

Year after year Hatfield struggled against each new escalation of the Vietnam War. Through both the Johnson and Nixon presidencies, Hatfield sacrificed support that might have come from the White House for other initiatives. In a number of ways Hatfield's struggles against the Vietnam War intensified his overall peace position. He declared himself to be a "Vietnam C.O. [conscientious objector]" and came very close to concluding that war should never again be supported. In the minds of many, the war radicalized the senator from Oregon, just as it radicalized a whole generation of young people.

Opposing most subsequent wars — Mark Hatfield continued to oppose U.S. involvement in most wars that occurred after Vietnam. He voted against the Democratic and Republican resolution authorizing the use of force in the 1991 Gulf War. He opposed President Clinton's decision to send U.S. troops to Bosnia. Only after his retirement from the Senate did he depart from this pattern by supporting President George W. Bush's decision to lead the United States into the Iraq

War. This action provides an interesting "bookend" image for his views on war, for he described the events of September 11, 2001, in New York and Washington as another Pearl Harbor, consisting of a direct attack on American soil and American citizens. He supported the expansion of the war in Iraq and endorsed the reelection campaign of President Bush. Taking that position shocked some of Hatfield's supporters and friends, but it underscores the point that he doesn't fit into the national nonviolence position that opposes *every* resort to war in defense of humanity.[12]

Seeking a balanced position on conflict in the Middle East — Hatfield visited Israel while he served as governor and again during his first term in the Senate. The latter time he made a point of going to several Palestinian refugee camps, as well as talking with political leaders from both Palestine and Israel. He felt troubled by the existence of the refugee camps and the semi-permanent despair of many who lived there. In remarks in the Senate he later asked his colleagues to pay more attention to the injustices suffered by Palestinians. "Our viewpoints must become sensitive to the injustice that Palestinians feel so deeply," he said. In a follow-up discussion with senators Aiken of Vermont and Hansen of Wyoming, Hatfield expressed regret that sympathetic expressions regarding the "other side" resulted in criticism. Many assumed that to be *for* the Palestinians in any way was to be *against* Israel, and vice versa.[13]

Also during this Senate discussion of 1970, Hatfield called on the United States to use its power, resources, and idealism to become a bona fide peacemaker between Israel and Palestine. A succession of Republican and Democratic presidents had placed most of their support behind the Israelis, fearing the possible alliance of Palestinians with other Arab states in the region. Continuing to call for an even-handed policy between Israel and Palestine earned Hatfield the distrust of some on both sides, for partisans on this issue echo those on abortion: They have a low tolerance for moderates who respect the validity of certain aspects of both points of view.[14]

Restricting the proliferation of nuclear weapons — The impact of his visit to Hiroshima never faded from Hatfield's consciousness. He saw the devastation firsthand. He met some of the survivors. From that time forward, "never again" seemed imprinted on his moral consciousness. After the United States began to withdraw from Vietnam, Hatfield took up the fight against nuclear weapons. He listened skeptically as Pentagon officials came to Capitol Hill to request funds for research, development, and procurement of new missile systems; new bombers; and exotic new weapons like the neutron bomb, designed to kill people while preserving buildings. He took advantage of his growing seniority and eventual chairmanship of the Senate Appropriations Committee to do what he could to stand in the way of funding nuclear weapons.

Hatfield's opposition to nuclear weapons converged with a growing citizen antinuclear-weapons movement. In 1957, Coretta Scott King, Albert Schweitzer, Benjamin Spock, and other prominent Americans formed a group called SANE, urging sanity with regard to the testing and production of nuclear weapons. Numerous Hollywood figures and other celebrities joined the cause. Hatfield agreed with SANE's position that the Anti-Ballistic Missile Treaty and Strategic Arms Limitation Treaty (SALT) agreement represented inadequate responses to the arms race. SANE and Hatfield also found common cause in the effort to stop the funding of the Vietnam War and to end the bombing in Cambodia.

In 1981 a young researcher on weapons issues took the lead in establishing a coalition of groups that aimed to freeze and reverse the nuclear arms race. Calling itself the Nuclear Weapons Freeze Campaign, the new group wanted the United States and U.S.S.R to agree to a mutual freeze on the production, testing, and deployment of nuclear weapons systems—especially the MX and Pershing II missiles. Hatfield joined Senator Ted Kennedy and Representative Pat Schroeder in pursuing the group's goals in Congress, and Hatfield and Kennedy coauthored a book on the subject. A year after its establishment, the Freeze Campaign organized a rally in New York City, drawing close to a million participants, making it what is said to be the largest such gathering up to that time. Numerous city governments and state legislatures endorsed the group's agenda, as did voters participating in state referenda.[15]

As the nuclear-freeze movement gained strength, Hatfield worked closely with organizations such as Pax Christi and the Fellowship of Reconciliation. He stayed in touch with the staff of *Sojourners* magazine, especially through Wes Granberg-Michaelson, who by then had become one of the magazine's editors. One surprising "convert" to the antinuclear-weapons cause during this time was evangelist Billy Graham, who after talking with Hatfield decided to preach against nuclear weapons—something that pleased the progressives and puzzled the conservatives.[16]

Appropriating Money for Defense — For one who didn't consider himself a pacifist, Senator Hatfield had an amazing voting record on defense spending bills. For a number of years he routinely voted against the bills, even though he chaired the committee that considered them. As amendments came up for consideration and as he discussed his views, he always made it clear that he wanted to provide adequate support for military personnel. He wanted American troops well-equipped and well-paid. His voting against the bills focused especially on the funding of various nuclear-weapons systems bills would authorize and later fund. He also tried to block the funding of research and development of new weapons systems, conventional or nuclear, especially those that carried enormous price tags but dubious value.

Fortunately for Hatfield, Oregon businesses had never participated significantly in the defense industry, so the senator didn't have to worry about the political consequences of his stand (as did the members of congressional delegations from the adjoining states of Washington and California, where substantial defense industries existed). Hatfield had no problem in taking a principled stand against excessive military spending *(see chapter 7)*.

Building Alternate Structures for Peace — As a long-time member of the Appropriations Committee, Hatfield became painfully aware of the excessive amounts spent each year on defense. He knew that his "no" vote would not change the eventual passage of the spending bills, but he wanted to take a stand against defense spending and to find a way to put a few resources into the search for peace. In 1984 he attached an amendment to a military appropriations bill that provided funding for the U.S. Institute of Peace, noting the irony of the legislative proximity between war and peace. The U.S. Institute was first called a "peace academy" to highlight the need to prepare individuals for peace, just as the military academies prepare individuals for war. But the peace institute became a grant-making and program agency, not an educational institution. To the surprise of many, it survived the skepticism of two conservative presidents and remains alive and well today.

Hatfield also favored the establishment of a Department of Peace at the cabinet level, even though he expressed misgivings about establishing yet another federal department and placing yet another cabinet member at the table. He also spoke about the need for something he called "Volunteers for Peace." He had admired the Peace

SEEKING PEACE AND JUSTICE

Corps and its mission of humanitarian and economic development, but he envisioned an entity that would recruit and deploy health-care professionals, technicians, and mediators into the conflict areas of the world to work for peaceful resolution of conflicts.[17]

Advocating for Justice — When Mark Hatfield talked about his ideals and convictions regarding peace, he frequently quoted Scripture and used the Hebrew word *shalom*. He also frequently used another Old Testament term that pointed to an important and often-overlooked dimension of peace, namely *justice*. Many peace groups today make a point of speaking of "peace with justice." The justice part of this pair of concepts concerns caring for those whom the wealthy and powerful overlook (or don't even see). These are the orphans, the widows, the refugees, the homeless, the sick, and the poor—exactly the groups highlighted in the Bible. Peacemaking can be construed as protecting the wealthy from violence and managing the finite resources (such as oil) that often lead to violent conflict. Justice means attending to the needy who can't return the favors of the prosperous.

Hatfield's emphasis on human justice, as understood from scriptural contexts, places him in the progressive zone of evangelicalism; but one also sees his conservative evangelical theology coming out in statements he often made about "sin," such as this one:

> Deprivation, suffering, hunger, alienation from God and man, lack of dignity, oppression—these strangle the world's hope for true peace. These are the obstacles to peace. True, they are perpetrated by sin—the sin of those who, absorbed by their wealth, power, privilege, and supposed self-righteousness, are blind to the responsibility of meeting these needs. Such sin is too often our own....We may attempt to enforce stability, or "law and order," through the use of force; but we will never have peace in our land until we repent from this sin, correct such injustice, and fulfill these needs.[18]

A Fully Developed Commitment to Peace and Justice

This overview makes it clear how Hatfield's initiatives and positions on peace and justice were central to his political philosophy and how they place him squarely in the category of progressive. Because so much of his work in the Senate took place in the Appropriations Committee, he

had many opportunities to advocate the shifting of funds into programs designed to nurture and protect human life, instead of endan-
gering it. To that theme we now turn.

7

BUTTER OR GUNS

In introductory economics courses students learn about the tradeoff between "guns and butter"—the idea that limited public resources cannot fully fund the goods and services demanded by both military and civilian groups. Often the guns-and-butter formulation functions as little more than a classroom exercise, but the concept actually had a central place in many of Mark Hatfield's congressional policy choices.

As a progressive, Hatfield felt drawn to the butter side of the equation. Yet as a combat veteran, he believed in the need to adequately provide for the needs of military personnel, without spending what he considered to be exorbitant sums for military hardware. During two periods of service as chair of the Senate Appropriations Committee, he had the opportunity to impact the choice between guns and butter. He regularly battled with Republican and Democratic administrations as they argued for what he considered an excessive supply of guns, feeling sure such military purchases would diminish the capacity to provide for the well-being of the poor and do little or nothing to preserve peace.

Meeting Human Needs

In a 1970 speech, Hatfield spoke of the need for government to provide adequately for human well-being. He urged his listeners to ground their views on New Testament concepts of compassion and justice, not on conservative fears about socialism, the welfare state, and big government.

In a speech to Pentagon employees a few months before, he criticized excessive spending on defense, which he said had grown to fifteen times the outlays for social and economic betterment. He challenged these civilian and military employees of the Defense Department to look beyond military readiness to the broader obstacles to global peace.

"A fundamental obstacle to peace, then," he said, "is the deprivation of mankind, both individually and corporately. There can be no peace within man, peace in his family, peace within our communities, and peace in the world until we fulfill the total needs of mankind."[1]

Hatfield often cited conservative authorities for the progressive points he wanted to make. For example, he noted the warnings of the conservative U.S. senator from Ohio, Robert A. Taft, that excessive military spending in peacetime is damaging to the economy. Hatfield agreed with Taft on this point and on Taft's non-interventionist position prior to Pearl Harbor, but not on many of Taft's extremely conservative positions on other issues. Hatfield also often mentioned the views of the man who in 1952 defeated Taft for the Republican nomination for president, Dwight D. Eisenhower, on the guns/butter question. Eisenhower once spoke of the use of resources it took to manufacture guns, ships, and rockets as outright theft from the needy of the world: "This world in arms is not spending money alone. It is spending the sweat of its laborers, the genius of its scientists, the hopes of its children."[2]

Virtually every time Hatfield challenged specific military spending proposals, he also made it clear he had no quarrel with maintaining a strong military, and in fact wanted those in uniform appropriately compensated and adequately equipped to carry out their missions.

When Hatfield did throw down the gauntlet in resisting defense spending, he said his goal was balance and propriety, not undermining the national defense capability. He intended to exercise his role as a responsible public official in challenging the blank checks he felt his colleagues in the Congress were willing to write for defense. He did not pretend that no threats existed to world peace, but he aimed to stand in the way of what he considered a reversal of the scriptural passage about pounding swords into plowshares.[3]

Difficult Choices

The opportunity to translate general principles into hard decisions on the guns/butter question came quickly in Hatfield's Senate career. Arriving in Congress burdened with skepticism about the Vietnam War, he took special note of the first military appropriations bill on which he had an opportunity to vote.

As a professor Hatfield had lectured on the constitutional division of powers, which gave Congress the "power of the purse." When he arrived in the Senate, it seemed particularly urgent that this power be exercised, since the Johnson administration had asserted it had no need to get Congressional approval for continuing and expanding the war in Southeast Asia. So why not vote against the funding measure that included Vietnam War money and thus send a message to the White House?

Unfortunately, the same appropriations bill that allocated money for bombs and napalm also provided for the men and women in uniform—for their salaries, their benefits, their nourishment, their ammunition, and spare parts for their equipment. Hatfield had even received a complaint from a Vietnam helicopter pilot that most of his unit's helicopters had stopped working for lack of spare parts.

Hatfield approached a senior colleague in the Senate, J. William Fulbright, a Democrat from Arkansas, inquiring how he deal with the dilemma of wanting to keep the troops well-equipped and also stay determined to pressure the president into backing away from an objectionable war. Hatfield considered casting a protest vote on the defense bill, reasoning that it would pass with or without his vote, but eventually decided against it. In remarks on the Senate floor, however, he criticized Defense Secretary Robert McNamara and the Defense Department for not finding enough in the $75 million daily outlays in Vietnam to properly equip and resupply the troops.[4]

The guns/butter theme came up constantly in Hatfield's anti-Vietnam War rhetoric during his first term in the Senate. He searched for a way to respond to the default position of many Americans, namely, that citizens should not criticize either the government's decision to initiate a war or question its conduct of the war.

Hatfield eventually countered this position with another conservative stand: The war was costing so much it was damaging the economy and further escalating the national debt. He used figures that seemed large at the time: $130 billion spent on the war as of 1967, one quarter of the nation's annual budget going to the war, and a price tag of $400,000 for each enemy soldier killed.

Hatfield also deplored the cuts in human-resource programs that resulted from increased defense spending. Millions of American children, he said, lived in families without enough money to visit the dentist. Millions of American adults found themselves trapped in poverty, with little hope of finding a job and no prospect of obtaining decent housing. Not only did the war drain the federal treasury, it also caused a serious "brain drain" of engineers and scientists, drawn away from important civilian projects.[5]

From Words to Action

Midway through his first term in the Senate, Hatfield moved beyond speaking out against war to taking concrete steps against it. This included using the power of the purse. Up to that time the Pentagon had enjoyed an open purse.

Hatfield joined forces with Democratic Senator George McGovern to try putting the brakes on the U.S. war effort *(see chapter 9)*. They sponsored a clear and dramatic amendment that called for cutting off funding for all but the orderly withdrawal of American troops. It directed that U.S. troops be withdrawn from Cambodia in 30 days, from Laos by the end of 1970, and Vietnam by mid-1971. The amendment failed to pass.

Hatfield later carried his guns/butter efforts into the committee that put spending at center stage, the Senate Appropriations Committee. When he came to the Senate, he had no real choice of committees. But in 1973 he succeeded in gaining a position on the Senate Appropriations Committee and from 1981 to 1987 (and again from 1995 to 1997) he served as chairman of that powerful committee. Even though the Vietnam War was nearing its end by the time he joined the committee, he knew the guns-and-butter issue would continue to occupy much of the group's work.

The funding of the B-1 bomber—a supersonic, long-range aircraft designed primarily to deliver nuclear weapons—typified the military procurement requests that came before Hatfield's committee.

Engineered in the late 1960s and flown for the first time a year after Hatfield joined the Appropriations Committee, the funding of the B-1 was the kind of weapons program he loved to hate.

Not only did the B-1 carry an astronomical price tag, it also clashed with Hatfield's conviction that nations built a strong military primarily by providing adequate numbers of military personnel and by providing superior training and equipment for them. Moreover, the airplane's direct connection to the nuclear program made it one of Hatfield's frequent targets for spending cuts, both within the Appropriations Committee and on the Senate floor.[6]

Respectful, Not Docile

As a junior Republican senator, Hatfield's opposition to various military spending initiatives did not pose a serious problem to the White House. In reality, Hatfield felt inclined to respect the men who served as president and his strong loyalty to the Republican Party reinforced that tendency when the commander in chief came from the GOP. But he regularly disagreed with the presidents, regardless of party, on issues of deep principle regarding spending choices.

In 1970 when Hatfield and Senator McGovern sought to bring a halt to the U.S. presence in Vietnam, Hatfield spoke out against Nixon's plan to veto an appropriations bill for health, education, and welfare programs. Nixon called the bill inflationary, but Hatfield said using the funds for human needs would use taxpayer money far more effectively than sending billions to a failed war effort.[7]

The stakes in Hatfield's opposition to military spending became much higher in 1981 when Ronald Reagan took the presidential oath of office. Republicans gained control of the Senate at the same time, making Hatfield the chair of the Senate Appropriations Committee. Hatfield's colleagues in the Senate had considered his many previous votes against appropriations bills a tolerable expression of his principles, but as chair of the funding committee, he had a much more substantial platform to express his convictions. His fellow Republicans expected him to oversee debate on appropriations bills and work for their passage. In this role Hatfield routinely consulted with President Reagan and other Senate leaders about initiatives the president hoped would make their way through the legislative process.

Hatfield chaired the Reagan inaugural ceremonies in January 1981 and genuinely admired the president. The Hatfields hosted the president and first lady at their Georgetown home for dinner and remained on good terms personally. But the senator never left any doubt about his feelings regarding Reagan's military programs.

Hatfield called the "star wars" anti-missile program a "terrifying proposal" and he fought hard against proposed funding for chemical-weapons programs. Hatfield characterized the Reagan defense programs as "technical nightmares, riddled with inefficiencies," and said they were "neither sound nor fiscally responsible." Eliminating any doubt about the depth of his feelings, Hatfield said Reagan was "about to shatter accepted notions of the impossible by attempting to save the Earth by militarizing space; eliminate nuclear weapons while producing them with abandon; and assuming that we will reduce the deficit in the process."[8]

At one regular White House meeting for Senate leaders, Hatfield had endured all he could of President Reagan's complaints about the rising federal deficit. He challenged Reagan's premise that blame for the unbalanced budget should be placed on the Appropriations Committee. Hatfield pointed out that the president's own spending requests had exceeded what Congress had approved, so if anyone was pushing up the deficit, it was the president. The point baffled Reagan and he turned to Secretary of Defense Casper Weinberger to comment. To Hatfield's amazement, Weinberger assured Reagan that military spending did not increase the federal deficit and that the problem actually lay with the social programs that Hatfield favored. Hatfield's Senate colleagues fully understood the inconsistency between Reagan's rhetoric about balancing the budget and his endless push for increased defense spending during peacetime. No one on Capitol Hill tried to argue that increasing defense spending did not increase the deficit.[9]

Hatfield once characterized Reagan's tactics on human service programs as "starving, choking, and evisceration." It saddened him that by the end of the Reagan presidency the United States was ranked 49th in the world in literacy, primarily because of its determination to remain the leader in spending for weapons.

Despite Reagan's success in persuading Congress and the American public to back his programs to strengthen the military, Hatfield looked back with some satisfaction on the eight years during which he and the president did battle on spending issues. He added up the successful cuts in defense spending that he had championed, and the total came to an impressive $100 billion. The money got redirected to things like education, job programs, and human needs initiatives—a tradeoff of butter for guns.[10]

Friends and Adversaries

John Stennis, Hatfield's Senate colleague, fellow Bible-study participant, and good friend, might have felt annoyed by Hatfield's antimilitary spending efforts, since Stennis chaired the Armed Services Committee. But when someone queried Stennis, a Democrat from Mississippi, about Hatfield's voting pattern on defense, he disputed the charge that Hatfield had taken an extreme position.

Stennis called Hatfield open and fair about the way he pursued his goals and insisted that his friend did not oppose the military. Stennis's generous assessment of Hatfield's voting record may have come in gratitude for Hatfield's 1973 decision to become a volunteer telephone operator and press officer at the hospital when Stennis nearly died after a mugging incident. With such a solid foundation for their friendship, the two men could understand and respect one another while voting in opposite ways on defense spending.[11]

A similar history of goodwill did not exist between Hatfield and one of his Republican colleagues in the Senate, Jesse Helms of North Carolina. From a distance it might have appeared that Helms and Hatfield had much more in common than did Stennis and Hatfield. After all, they were both Republicans and both Christians. But Hatfield's evangelical progressivism and Helms's Christian fundamentalism led the two men to very different views on defense spending. One of Hatfield's former staff members recalled an example of the difficulties in the Helms-Hatfield working relationship.

Hatfield once sought votes on the Senate floor against a measure providing funding for "nerve gas," a chemical substance sometimes used in combat but eventually banned by the Chemical Weapons Convention of 1993. Nerve gasses, such as sarin, either cause a rapid and painful death or permanent neurological damage. Hatfield asked Helms for his support for the measure and Helms agreed.

But when Helms' plan to vote against nerve gas became known on the Senate floor, fellow Senate hawks were aghast that Helms would side with Hatfield on the issue and persuaded him to change his vote. Reneging on one's word like this to a Senate colleague was considered an egregious breach of collegiality.[12] The flip-flop by Helms led to the defeat of Hatfield's effort, since Vice President Bush broke a resulting tie in favor of the nerve-gas funding.

Working for More Butter

As his experience and staffing strength on the Appropriations Committee grew, Hatfield devoted as much energy to funding butter as he did to opposing spending for guns. He especially worked for more adequate funding for medical research and health care, education, and transportation.

Hatfield often pointed to the "multiplier" effect this kind of spending tended to produce. He asserted, for example, that every dollar spent on medical research ultimately generated $50 in benefits within the research-and-health-care system, as well as increased productivity, as successful treatments for diseases cut down on employees' time away from work.

While funding for the development and production of weapons systems also added jobs, the multiplier was much less. Scientists and engineers got paid for the design phase and production workers earned their paychecks in the defense industries, but the deployment of missiles, airplanes, and bombs brought an end to the economic chain of benefits. The hardware might have a deterrent benefit and might occasionally get used in combat, but economists regularly demonstrated the disappointing economic growth associated with military production.[13]

Oregon Butter

As already noted, Oregon had nothing like the massive defense factories operated around the country by such firms as Lockheed Martin, Grumman, Raytheon, and General Dynamics. Boeing, based at the time in the Seattle area, had a small operation in Portland, but it did not account for many jobs and emphasized civilian aircraft production more than defense. This fact freed up Hatfield to focus on the funding of butter in Oregon and he did so with zeal.

In his reelection campaigns of 1984 and 1990, Hatfield looked back on several years as chair or ranking Republican on the Senate Appropriations Committee—and pointed to projects that he believed benefited not only Oregon, but the entire country. Hatfield saw the issue of local vs. national benefit as sensitive, since many of the projects he shepherded through the Appropriations Committee had the appearance of benefiting only the local communities where the funded items were built.

Port facilities along the Oregon coast and the Columbia River, for example, regularly needed federal help with dredging and rebuilding the river channels leading to the docks. Some might have labeled such funding "pork barrel" projects, the derogatory term favored by everyone except the advocates and beneficiaries of the funded projects. One could picture a person with Hatfield's power having a large barrel of money at hand for constituent groups who showed up for yet another public works project in their part of the state. Yet despite his progressive outlook, Hatfield also considered himself a fiscal conservative, so he felt sensitive to charges stating he stood ready to reach into the pork barrel whenever his state needed money.

Had doling out of the pork been his real goal, Hatfield could have patterned his career after a skilled practitioner of the art, Warren Magnuson, Democrat from Washington. Hatfield had served on the Appropriations Committee with Magnuson from 1972 to 1981. Some observers claimed that Magnuson made sure many "monuments" got erected in the state of Washington—evidences of his power when he was chair of the committee.

Hatfield disliked the term *pork*, preferring to think of spending as the legitimate allocation of public funds. He believed his constituents expected him to use his seniority in the appropriations process to ensure their projects received fair consideration, and when appropriate, sufficient funding. He directed committee staff members—many from Oregon—to consult with local agencies to assure that these projects received fair considerations in the battle for competing funds.

In some cases, staffers justified proposed projects primarily on the basis of community or regional needs. A flood-control project on a state river, for example, might have national benefit only in the context of preventing disasters that could generate larger demands for federal funds.

Hatfield also backed many projects built and operated in Oregon on the basis that they could point the way to addressing public needs in other parts of the country. The senator had a great deal to do with the funding of Portland's light-rail transportation system, ably assisted in the House of Representatives by Les AuCoin, a Democrat representing the west side of the Portland metropolitan area. The pair argued in favor of federal investment in the project to demonstrate how such a system could address air quality problems in urban areas even as it helped to conserve the nation's dwindling supply of oil.

When federal funds flowed to his state, Hatfield frequently pointed out that Oregon did not benefit heavily from federal funding. Nearly half of the state's land is publicly owned, most of it under federal management. Management of public land generates some income to the federal government in the form of timber sales, grazing fees, and recreational fees, but these revenues go mostly toward land management. Oregon has what might be called a negative balance of revenue—more federal taxes flowing out of the state than federal funds flowing back in. So Hatfield felt only mildly apologetic when an Oregon project made it through his committee.

Projects associated with the Oregon Health & Science University (OHSU), located near the Veterans Administration hospital in Portland, represented the most dramatic concentration of Oregon appropriations that Hatfield supported on the grounds of national benefit. With Hatfield's urging, the federal government made substantial sums of federal money available for funding medical-research programs at OHSU. A steady stream of witnesses from around the country came to Congress, pleading for funding to initiate and accelerate research into the diseases that affected them and their families. Through Hatfield's efforts, Congress funded a number of these research programs, with some research institutes established in Portland.

Hatfield's own father became one of thousands of Alzheimer's victims in Oregon, giving the senator a personal motivation to do what he could for research into the causes and treatment of the disease. Today the Aging and Alzheimer's Disease Center at OHSU exists largely because of Hatfield's work to fund it. But he did not restrict the funding to Oregon; a total of 30 such research centers exist around the country, assisted and coordinated by the National Institute on Aging.

Most of the programs Hatfield helped fund in Oregon do not carry his name. One exception is the Hatfield Marine Science Center in Newport, Oregon, operated by Oregon State University. Hatfield worked mostly for the funding of the less-visible human service programs that would benefit the region and the nation. Hatfield found personal satisfaction in his time in office by looking to the "monuments" of nationally significant butter projects.

Shifting the Balance

If during his time in office Mark Hatfield had concentrated only on reducing national spending on guns, he would have left a legacy of moderately successful obstructionism. But when his Appropriations Committee came to the floor with yet another measure containing substantial sums for health care and research, a chorus of support usually arose from his colleagues, eager to endorse the butter. And for that, a few monuments did get erected.

After he retired from the Senate, colleagues named a human service facility in suburban Washington, D.C., in the senator's honor, the Mark O. Hatfield Clinical Research Center at the National Institutes of Health.

Throughout his legislative career, Hatfield worked to shift the balance from guns to butter. Much of his zeal to reduce excessive military spending came from his early struggles against the Vietnam War. It is to that polarizing conflict that we now direct our attention.

8

A GOVERNOR AND THE VIETNAM WAR

Mark Hatfield's interest in Vietnam began long before his spiritual worldview began shaping his political positions as a public official. His interest in the war also began long before American officials took the first steps toward involving the United States in the region.

This interest, along with his concern about war as a moral issue and nuclear weapons as a vivid case of human evil, came from his personal experience in World War II. And his growing concern about Vietnam drew him into national debate during his last term as governor in a way he probably hadn't expected. In fact, it put his future political goals at considerable risk.

A Grim Introduction to Vietnam

Hatfield's experiences during World War II profoundly affected his thinking about global politics. We have already considered his experiences at Iwo Jima and Hiroshima *(see chapter 6)*. Another key experience took place far outside the main combat areas of the Pacific theater. A brief visit to Vietnam permanently changed the way Hatfield saw that part of the world.

While French officials in the late-18th century had given help to one side in a civil conflict in Indochina, the local people showed little gratitude, harassing and killing many Vietnamese converts to Christianity. With the encouragement of other European Catholic nations, France landed troops in 1858 to protect the Christians. Three decades later it formed the colony of French Indochina from the separate components of what is now Vietnam, the Khmer Republic, and Laos.

Indigenous resistance to French occupation continued for many years. Japan, motivated by its opposition to non-Asian imperialism (as well as by its own colonial ambitions) gave some assistance to these nationalist efforts. In 1940 Japan occupied Indochina as part of its expansion in Asia. It put its own officials in charge but did not remove the Vichy French administrators still loyal to Germany. This left the people of Indochina with a triple colonial curse: The Japanese, already well on their way to controlling the Pacific; the remnants of French rule, including many powerful French business people; and a puppet emperor, Bao Dai, who remained loyal to the Japanese. A better incubator for anti-colonialism is hard to imagine.

As might be expected, a local leader eventually emerged to organize resistance to outside control, well before the Japanese empire fell apart. This leader, Ho Chi Minh, had learned well the lessons of radical nationalism. Before World War I, Minh had made his way to Europe as a cabin boy. After the war he settled in Paris and became a founding member of the French Communist Party.

Minh later spent considerable time in Moscow, learning about Soviet communism, and with Soviet encouragement returned to Indochina in 1941. He then joined and ultimately became the leader of the Viet Minh, a local nationalist movement initially founded to organize resistance against the Japanese. With some help from the United States and China, the Viet Minh grew stronger during the war, but never became as powerful as either the Japanese or the French.[1]

After the war, Japan's surrender of control in the north of Indochina left many unsolved problems. On the one hand, the Japanese conceded some legitimacy to the Democratic Republic of Vietnam that Ho Chi Minh and the Viet Minh established there in August, 1945. But this government had rivals for its claims, first from the Chinese Nationalist army sent to repatriate Japanese troops, and also from the Vichy French officials—allies of the Japanese. This three-way power struggle ultimately devolved into a direct conflict between the representatives of the postwar government in France and the Viet Minh. This conflict became the French Indochinese War that lasted for nearly a decade.

Mark Hatfield got a brief exposure to this political mess during his final days of service in the Navy. Hatfield's ship anchored in Haiphong harbor to pick up soldiers of the Chinese Nationalist army, who had overseen the demilitarization of Japanese troops. The Chinese had orders to go to northern China to fight the Chinese communists—an important part of the postwar power realignment.

The World War II political division between the Axis powers and the Allies quickly turned into a struggle between the Soviets and their communist allies on one side against various regional anticommunist coalitions on the other. Yet Hatfield had less interest in the place of Vietnam in this new East-West global alignment than he did in the human suffering and injustice he observed there.

While Hatfield's ship lay at anchor he took note of the local people, most of whom seemed desperately hungry. A terrible famine had swept parts of Indochina, caused by insufficient rains and poor crops as well as the hardships associated with Japanese occupation. Hatfield and his fellow sailors knew nothing of the crop failures, but they clearly saw the results. They witnessed famished and desperate people, scrambling to collect the garbage dumped from the ship and skirmishing over a few grains of rice spilled when the Americans loaded their supplies. In a letter to his parents, Hatfield blamed the French for the suffering he witnessed. He spoke of the French as the worst agents of enslavement in the West's "mad desire for money." And stories about wealthy French patrons of Hanoi casinos who totally disregarded the hunger around them made him both sad and angry.[2]

The Domino Theory

Hatfield's impressions of his visit to Indochina remained largely dormant during his graduate studies, teaching years, and his early involvement in state and local politics. During this time developments in Indochina grew ominous, but not serious enough to get noticed by most Americans.

Ho Chi Minh had appointed Bao Dai, the powerless emperor of Indochina during Japanese occupation, to advise his new government in the north, the Democratic Republic of Vietnam. Meanwhile, Japanese forces in southern Indochina surrendered to British officers as part of the Allied demilitarization plan. The British sought help from officials of the new French government in an effort to establish control over the Viet Minh and other indigenous political and religious factions. This turned out to be far more difficult than the British and

French had imagined, and the French ultimately lost their nine-year war, suffering a decisive defeat in the battle of Dien Bien Phu. The French subsequently withdrew from Indochina under the terms of the Geneva Accords and also recognized Ho Chi Minh's Democratic Republic of Vietnam.

The situation in the south, however, turned in a very different direction. Near the end of the French Indochina War, the United States had become increasingly involved in the area and had participated in the Geneva peace talks. American officials felt a growing concern about the outcome of the Korean War of 1950-1953, which had left a communist government firmly in control of the north. Advocates of the "domino theory" warned that another communist victory in Asia would mean losing the entire region to communism.

In response to the threat the western allies decided to install a constitutional monarchy in the south of Vietnam, with the former emperor Bao Dai as king and the anticommunist Ngo Dinh Diem as prime minister. Unfortunately, the United States refused to accept a major provision of the Geneva Accords that called for national elections and unification of the north and south under a new government. As a consequence, the "temporary" division of Indochina at the 17th parallel became artificially permanent. The Eisenhower administration had the dubious distinction of establishing the first U.S. military presence in South Vietnam, while a succession of Democratic and Republican presidents strengthened the American effort to keep the communists from dominating all of Vietnam.

During the late-1950s Hatfield concentrated on his duties at Willamette University and on his service as a member of the Oregon legislature, not on global politics. He, like most Americans, paid little attention to the increasing commitment of U.S. personnel as "advisors" in Vietnam. President John F. Kennedy picked up where Eisenhower left off in 1961, but directed more of his energy to responding to the Soviet threat in Cuba and elsewhere. Along with a majority of Americans, Kennedy worried about the "domino theory" and declared that Ho Chi Minh could not be allowed to take over all of Indochina.

Hatfield had strongly supported President Eisenhower and therefore did not become concerned about the early U.S. involvement in Indochina. Over time, however, he grew increasingly skeptical about

Kennedy's policies in Southeast Asia. This concern gave birth to a position that would shape his political life for well over a decade.

Not a Prudent Move

In later years Hatfield stated that he did not take a stand against U.S. involvement in Vietnam for political reasons. On the contrary, he said, his stance was far from a prudent political move for a successful Republican governor with aspirations to national office. Rather, his opposition to American involvement in Vietnam came from two other sources.

The first source he called an intuitive, emotional sense of the wrongness of the U.S. intervention in Vietnam. Perhaps this feeling had roots in his vivid memories of visiting Indochina in 1945 and his strong belief that no outside political power would do any better than France in trying to determine for the Indochinese their political future.

The second source of Hatfield's opposition to the war had spiritual roots. After his life-changing spiritual awakening in the mid-1950s, Hatfield became increasingly vocal about his Christian faith. During his time as governor he talked with growing ease about what it meant to be a follower of Christ. Years later as he looked back on his decision to speak out against U.S. policies in Vietnam, he said it came down to a matter of remaining faithful to what he believed God wanted him to do. He said he felt a deep inner peace once he decided to proceed down this pathway and had no hesitation about accepting the political consequences of taking such a difficult direction.[3]

Hatfield later framed his decision in the context of just-war theology. He told a seminary audience that the means used to pursue a just war must remain consistent with the ends pursued. He spoke in particular of the My Lai Massacre in which American soldiers killed and injured hundreds of unarmed Vietnamese villagers. This episode, in combination with other distasteful aspects of the conflict, made it clear to him that Vietnam did not meet the criteria of a "just war."[4]

More Zeal than Caution

If Governor Hatfield's opposition to the Vietnam War had a political motivation, his choice of venue for his first major statement on the war, the Republican National Convention, would seem a particularly poor one.

In 1964 Lyndon Johnson was well on his way to winning the Democratic presidential nomination, hoping to receive a stronger mandate after completing the term of assassinated President Kennedy. Normally, any policy of the opposing party is considered fair game for criticism at its rival's national convention; given that Johnson had steadily escalated U.S. participation in Vietnam, Republicans had every right to criticize his policy. But in 1964 most Republicans fully agreed with the Democrats that communism had to be stopped in Southeast Asia. Moreover, this Republican convention appeared ready to nominate a conservative of conservatives, Barry Goldwater.

We have already noted how Hatfield used his keynote address at the convention to strongly criticize ultraconservatives associated with the John Birch Society *(see chapter 3)*. He spoke with sadness about American soldiers dying in a war without a name. He spoke of the tomb of the unknown soldier and lamented that thousands of "unknowing" soldiers had received no rationale for the war in Indochina and had little hope that it would come to a successful end—strong words before an audience not very interested in changing this part of U.S. foreign policy.[5]

After the convention Hatfield exercised more zeal than caution in selecting venues for his Vietnam message. His next speech about the war was at an American Legion convention in Oregon. Without specifically using just-war language, he used its principles as the basis for his criticism of the war, labeling the bombing of nonmilitary targets as alien to both Judeo-Christian and American moral values. He called on the administration to attend to the human needs that made the people of Vietnam so susceptible to the rhetoric of radical nationalists. And he expressed the hope that the United Nations would play an invited role in the quest for peace in Southeast Asia.[6]

Standing Alone Among the Governors

Governor Hatfield next tackled his fellow governors in a courageous effort to stand in the way of their unanimous support for the war. In the months between Lyndon Johnson's election and the national governors' conference in Minneapolis in the summer of 1965, Hatfield had become more and more disturbed about the steady commitment of troops, weapons, and funding for an undeclared war with a dubious objective and no hope of victory. His growing conviction about the futility of involvement in Vietnam put him on a crash course with the Johnson administration, which saw the governors' conference as an excellent opportunity to gather support for its efforts in Vietnam. Johnson already had received backing from business and labor groups and not only wanted the governors' support, but wanted that support to be unanimous.

Johnson spared no effort and expense to get the governors' backing. Vice President Hubert Humphrey put the proposal before the gathering, ignoring the fact that these state executives had no mandate for taking positions on foreign policy. The day after Humphrey's presentation, the supporting governors asked that the conference recess to hear President Johnson's statement to the American people about the Vietnam War. When the president concluded his remarks, Georgia governor Carl Sanders put forward a resolution endorsing Johnson's goals in Vietnam; soon it became apparent that the resolution had overwhelming support.

Only Hatfield raised questions. He asked proponents to clarify the nature of the commitment implied in the resolution. He warned that the Vietnam conflict could become like a march through quicksand, demanding ever more resources and becoming more and more difficult to escape.[7]

Everyone knew the resolution would pass, but would the administration get the unanimous vote it wanted? Governor George Romney of Michigan asked the governors to delay the vote until after they all met with the president the next day in Washington. Unwilling to take a chance that his vice president would succeed in persuading all the governors to vote for the resolution, Johnson had arranged to have the group flown to the nation's capital on Air Force One. A voice vote taken before the trip yielded a great many "ayes," a solid "no" from Governor Hatfield, and a weak "no" from Governor Romney. Some of Hatfield's colleagues later expressed admiration for his courage but puzzlement that he would take such a political risk in opposing a war with such widespread national support.

President Johnson pulled out all the stops during his White House meeting with the governors. A parade of cabinet members, military officers, and staff members laid out the case for the war, seeking to persuade a group of governors who already had passed a pro-war resolution with only two dissenting votes. As the session concluded, Governor Romney announced his satisfaction with the case made for the legitimacy of the Vietnam War.

With only one governor standing between Johnson and unanimous passage, the president turned to Governor Hatfield to ask if he had any questions. Hatfield responded that he had no questions, but neither did he have any intention of supporting the war. Johnson immediately proposed that Hatfield talk with reporters about his position, hoping the governor would bend under the national media pressure and change his views. But the tactic failed; Hatfield declined the opportunity to face the media, remained steadfast in his convictions, and went on his way.[8]

The annual governors' conference in the summer of 1966 in Los Angeles featured a replay of events from the same gathering a year earlier. Republican governors caucused and tried to think of a way to keep the war off the agenda, but the Democrats had no intention of letting that happen. Texas governor John Connally handled the issue on the floor of the conference.

This time Hatfield faced higher stakes. He had won the Republican nomination to the U.S. Senate and the time was short until the general election. If foreign policy had little consequence for Hatfield as governor, the same could not be said of Hatfield the candidate for U.S. Senate; and the Democratic nominee, Robert Duncan, had decided to make the Vietnam War a major issue in the campaign.

The war resolution at the 1966 governors' conference brought more extensive debate than it had the year before. Proponents tried to generate support for it by including words affirming the patriotism of those serving in uniform. Hatfield said he certainly wanted to commend American troops, but couldn't accept the resolution's language about "global commitments," without any details explaining the extent of such commitments. He proposed wording that included support for the troops, but left out the more ambiguous language of support for the president. His effort failed and several governors urged Hatfield either to support the resolution as written or "take a walk" during the voting, thus assuring a unanimous vote.

While congressional voting sometimes involves intentional absenteeism, the spotlight on Hatfield the previous year made it impossible for him to sit this one out, even if he wanted to. At the end of the discussion the governors took a roll call vote, perhaps intending to put even greater pressure on Hatfield. But once more he cast the only contrary vote.[9]

On to the Senate

As Hatfield completed his final year as chief executive of Oregon and busied himself with his Senate campaign, he had to face the political consequences of his unpopular position on the Vietnam War. He had to wonder: *Did I make the right choice?*

As an evangelical Christian, however, he felt called to continue his opposition to the war; as a progressive, he knew he could not remain silent while the government drained the federal treasury to fund a war he considered deeply wrong.

9

THE VIETNAM WAR IN THE SENATE

Political advisors and critics alike might have counseled Mark Hatfield not to vote against the governors' resolution supporting U.S. activities in Vietnam *(discussed in chapter 8)*. But on this issue and others Hatfield generally followed the advice of his father: to stand alone, when necessary, on matters of deeply held principle.

Hatfield would not have won six Oregon elections in a row if he lacked talent as a political strategist. But a more risk-averse candidate certainly would have stayed away from the 1966 governors' conference or stifled his or her objections to the Vietnam resolution. By the time Hatfield got to that point his stand on the war had become a serious political problem.

The First Senate Campaign

Hatfield's decision to run for the U.S. Senate in 1966 seemed like a "no brainer." Oregonians had elected Maurine Neuberger to serve out the remainder of her late husband's term as senator, and they elected her for another full term after that. But incumbent senator Maurine Neuberger had decided against running for a second full term, thus leaving the seat open. Neuberger's decision put Hatfield in an ideal situation.

As the first Oregon governor in that century to serve two full terms in office, Hatfield had earned very high name recognition in the state. His stand on Vietnam, however, cast an ominous political cloud over his campaign prospects. A reputable local polling firm conducted an opinion study just after the governors' conference, showing that more than three-fourths of Oregonians supported the Vietnam War and that almost a third of that number favored strengthening the American military commitment there. Fewer than one in six said they thought the United States should get out of Vietnam—the position Hatfield had taken.

The state's strongest daily newspaper, the sponsor of the poll, editorialized that although Hatfield had become the most popular politician in the state, he risked becoming an ex-politician as a result of his unpopular stand on Vietnam. In such a political climate, Hatfield's most trusted advisors urged him to concentrate on noncontroversial issues such as natural resources, while downplaying his stand on Vietnam.[1]

Advisors to the Democratic nominee, U.S. congressman Robert Duncan—who had been a member of the Oregon House while Hatfield served in the Oregon Senate and as governor—took note of the sentiments of Oregon voters and urged Duncan to seek every opportunity to broadcast his support of continued U.S. engagement in Vietnam. Duncan pulled out all the stops in his support of President Johnson's position on Vietnam, banking on it as Hatfield's greatest vulnerability. But Duncan eventually overplayed his hand on this issue, giving voice to an extreme and less-than-credible version of the domino theory. He warned that failing to fight the enemy in Southeast Asia would eventually mean fighting them in the Northwest—something few of his fellow hawks considered a real threat.[2]

Hatfield did not sidestep the Vietnam issue in his Senate campaign, against the advice of some of his staff members. But he did try to broaden the range of issues debated. While he knew Oregon had a relatively strong economy at the time, he also knew that the forest products and agriculture industries lacked the strength to carry the state into future prosperity. So he emphasized his initiatives as governor to diversify the state's economy, while warning that the Johnson administration's heavy spending—especially for the escalating Vietnam War—put the economies of the state and nation at risk.

Although Duncan had chosen the more popular position on the Vietnam War, Hatfield won three statewide elections prior to his Senate campaign, which gave him tremendous experience in connecting with voters in the cities, towns, and rural areas of every part of the state. Congressman Duncan came from Medford, a small town near the southern border of Oregon, which meant that his two campaigns for the U.S. House had not introduced him to the rest of the state. Also, Duncan's profession as an attorney was one that many people love to hate.

As a member of the House of Representatives, Duncan also had to spend a great deal of time in Washington, attending to his duties 3,000 miles from Oregon. And as Oregon members of Congress learn quickly, it takes a long time to get from Washington, D.C., to Oregon. Nevertheless, Oregonians expect their representatives and senators to show up to vote in Congress, so Duncan found himself in a bind during the campaign.

Meanwhile, Hatfield fulfilled his promise to complete two full terms as governor. He could carry on his governmental duties while still making regular campaign appearances—the kind of campaign that had always "worked" for him. He traveled systematically and relentlessly to every community in the state, relying on an impressive network of volunteers in each county and town. These volunteers advised Hatfield about arranging useful and productive speaking opportunities in their areas and did their part to assure good turnout.

Polls in August showed Duncan leading by six points, which confirmed that Hatfield's strong political reputation in the state had enabled Duncan to overcome the Vietnam problem. While this gave hope to Duncan's supporters, it also motivated Hatfield's backers; they knew they still had time to turn the situation around.

Meanwhile, the potential for a Democratic upset of a veteran Republican politician attracted national Democratic leaders to Oregon to endorse Congressman Duncan. President Lyndon Johnson spent several days in Oregon expressing strong support for Duncan, whose loyalty on the Vietnam issue rivaled that of anyone in Congress. Johnson also still felt angry over Hatfield's unwillingness to grant him the unanimous pro-war vote he wanted from the governors in 1965 and 1966. Former Attorney General and Democratic senator Robert Kennedy also supported Duncan. But Kennedy's visit provided a mixed blessing to the Duncan campaign, for Kennedy opposed the president on the war and made no effort to hide his sentiments while in Oregon.

No one of the stature of Johnson or Kennedy came to Oregon to endorse Hatfield, but former Vice President Richard Nixon came from California to speak for Hatfield. *Time* magazine called the politicians' visits a "monsoon of out-of-state luminaries," but these visits did more to call attention to the importance of the race than to tip the balance one way or the other.[3]

In close and aggressively contested campaigns, significant numbers of voters often abandon their plans to cast a protest vote on a particular issue and instead support the candidate whose overall record they admire. Such proved to be the case in this contest, as Hatfield won the election with 51.7 percent of votes cast—a margin of only 24,000 votes. It became the closest race of his entire career. Still, his willingness to support unpopular positions meant he would have a number of other close races in the future.[4]

Carrying the Vietnam Issue into the Senate

On New Years Day, 1967—well before getting sworn in as a U.S. senator—Hatfield appeared on ABC's *Issues and Answers* program. Predictably, the questions he fielded dealt almost entirely with Vietnam.

The final question asked whether he intended to continue to emphasize his antiwar position as a member of the Senate. Hatfield threw caution to the wind and said he most assuredly would. Yet early in his time in Washington he found it difficult to accomplish much on this and other issues. As a new member with no seniority, he had to work in a crowded, temporary space. He also had to contend with the shock of transitioning from his role as CEO of a state to finding himself at the bottom of the food chain in the Senate.

While getting his bearings in Washington, Hatfield made a point of expressing support for the families of military personnel. In one instance he heard of a constituent serving in the Navy whose wife suffered from leukemia. He intervened to get the man a hardship discharge.

But not all of his constituents responded favorably to the senator's expressions of concern. One Oregonian returned, unopened, Hatfield's letter of condolence regarding the death of the man's son in Vietnam. An accompanying note blamed Hatfield for the young man's death. Unwilling to let the matter drop, Hatfield asked the director of his Oregon office, John Oberdorf—a World War II veteran and retired Air Force colonel—to help. Oberdorf drove from Salem to Eugene to find the bereaved father and assure him that Senator Hatfield empathized with his anguish. When he stopped to ask for directions to the man's home, Colonel Oberdorf was surprised to find that he was speaking to the person he had come to see. The man's hostility and caution was obvious, but his tone softened as he listened to Colonel Oberdorf and pondered the fact that a U.S. senator had sent a staff member to express his personal condolences.[5]

During his first year in the Senate, Hatfield found some support on the Vietnam issue from J. William Fulbright, Democrat from Arkansas. Fulbright had served for many years as chairman of the Senate Foreign Relations Committee, and in 1964 voted with the majority in favor of the Gulf of Tonkin Resolution. The resolution, prompted by a report that two Navy destroyers had been attacked by North Vietnam, gave considerable latitude to the president in expanding American military activities in Southeast Asia. Only two senators voted against the resolution, including Senator Wayne Morse of Oregon.

Two years later Fulbright took the side of Vietnam War critics in his book *The Arrogance of Power*. Fulbright chided Congress for failing to place limits on the administration's pursuit of the war, and his position as chair of the Foreign Relations Committee gave his message particular force. In late 1967 he went a step further, introducing a resolution requiring congressional action before the president could send troops into future conflicts. Hatfield supported the resolution, although he felt disappointed by its nonbinding character and especially that it would apply only to future conflicts. In any event, the resolution did not pass.[6]

Despite struggling to become familiar with the rules and procedures of "the Senate club" during his first year in office, Hatfield also undertook the ambitious task of writing his first book, *Not Quite So Simple*. The book became an important means of articulating his case against the Vietnam War. Nearly half of the book focused on Vietnam and provided an important sequel to Fulbright's book. By considering some of the book's key points, one can sense the intensity of Hatfield's convictions about the war:

- Questions about the validity of the war expressed one's patriotism, not treason. The assertion that debating the merits of the war helped the enemy had no basis in fact.

- The tactics used in the war violated historic legal and moral criteria for the conduct of war—tactics of destroying vegetation with Agent Orange, using napalm to burn homes, and bombing civilian areas.

- The Johnson administration had deceived the American people by promising in 1964 that it would not expand the land war or bomb in the north; after the election, it implemented precisely these measures.

- The administration had deliberately misrepresented the war as a response to aggression from the north, even though most of the energy for fighting the Americans came from the south.

- While Americans wanted to think of the war as a struggle to protect democracy, the government of South Vietnam was anything but democratic.

- Defeating Ho Chi Minh and the Vietcong would not bring peace, since multiple injustices in the south would stand in the way of genuine peace.

- The Geneva Accords provided for national elections, but the United States allowed the South Vietnamese government to avoid holding elections.

- Bombing in the north had not reduced the flow of supplies to the south, since China and Russia steadily replaced the destroyed material.

- Although the administration said it stood willing to participate in peace talks, it had not responded to peace overtures from the north.

- The United States was repeating the same mistake in Vietnam it had made elsewhere in the world, focusing on stability rather than on reform and justice.

- By its stubborn continuation of the war, the United States jeopardized its standing in global politics, particularly its relationship with the Soviet Union and China.

Hatfield delivered speeches about the Vietnam War to myriad groups during his first year in the Senate, drawing on the ideas he had expressed in his book. Then early in 1968 Hatfield began to look for a way to pursue the issue in the Senate. He hoped new developments in the conflict might generate—in Congress and among the American people—greater support for his position. The Tet Offensive demonstrated the strength of North Vietnam and the Vietcong, while North

Korea's seizure of the "Pueblo," a U.S. intelligence ship, also showed the strength of North Vietnam's allies.

Hatfield first drafted a Vietnam resolution with a relatively modest scope, directing the president to fully consult with Congress before extending the ground war beyond South Vietnam. In his introductory remarks he asserted that Congress had failed to exercise its responsibility to participate in making decisions about the war. He also made a point of not seeking cosponsors for the resolution, knowing that many who might ultimately support the measure would not want to declare themselves in advance. But his tactics were in vain; the resolution received little support and his efforts failed.[7]

Hatfield, Nixon, and the Vietnam War

In view of Hatfield's increasingly visible and vocal opposition to the war in Vietnam, an interesting development occurred in the 1968 presidential campaign involving antiwar Democratic candidate Eugene McCarthy. Hatfield had expressed informal support for McCarthy, but as a loyal Republican he had no inclination to pursue this sympathy very far. As the nominating convention approached he thought about his choices. Some assumed he would get behind moderate Republican Nelson Rockefeller, with whom he agreed on a number of issues. But Hatfield was not ready to do that.

Even though Rockefeller had criticized President Johnson about some aspects of his handling of the war, Hatfield seriously doubted that Rockefeller would act much differently than Johnson. As noted earlier, Hatfield and other Republican senators met with Rockefeller during the primaries to determine if they might feel ready to support him, but Hatfield disliked Rockefeller's response to questions he asked about Vietnam (see chapter 3). Hatfield also felt certain that Rockefeller's foreign policy advisor, Henry Kissinger, would urge Rockefeller toward continued engagement in Vietnam.

Meanwhile, in the early summer of 1968, Richard Nixon asked to meet with Hatfield to discuss his possible support. Nixon hoped that the friendship the two had developed might help him gain the backing of the senator from Oregon. They agreed on a number of mainstream Republican principles and even in their discussion of Vietnam, Nixon appeared to support Hatfield's insistence that addressing the human needs of South Vietnam took priority over trying to stamp out communism. Yet neither in his private meeting with Hatfield nor in any of his campaign statements did Nixon reveal how he would deal with the war.

Nixon's noncommittal position bothered Hatfield, but in an article published in *Christianity and Crisis*, he endorsed Nixon. Hatfield reasoned that Hubert Humphrey, the likely Democratic nominee, would fully pursue the Johnson policies, while Nixon might not. With no assurance that Rockefeller would handle the war any differently than Humphrey, Hatfield opted for supporting Nixon, holding on to the hope that Nixon would eventually move toward getting the United States out of Vietnam.[8]

As noted in chapter 3, Hatfield felt both disappointment and relief when Nixon passed him over in selecting a running mate. Nevertheless, Hatfield agreed to give speeches supporting Nixon, especially before audiences of university students, where Hatfield as a former professor felt some rapport. But many of the antiwar students doubted Nixon would be a better choice than Humphrey with regard to the Vietnam issue. As the election approached, Hatfield became frustrated with Nixon's unwillingness to make a commitment on Vietnam, and wrote him a letter saying so. The letter didn't change anything, but it did bring an end to the invitations for Hatfield to be a surrogate speaker in the Nixon campaign.[9]

Meanwhile Hatfield authored an article for the September-October issues of the moderate Republic publication *Ripon Forum*, challenging both candidates to more clearly articulate their positions on Vietnam. He didn't mention Nixon by name, but said neither candidate had given details on the question. He could have asked the publication not to run the article prior to the election; that would have coincided with his instincts as a party loyalist. But his progressive opposition to the war prevailed, and he let the article hit the newsstands before the election.

Hatfield's article, coupled with the comments he made after the election about Nixon's position on the war, earned him a "woodshed" session with Nixon's new secretary of state, William Rogers. Rogers asked Hatfield to refrain from open criticism of the administration while the administration worked out the details of its Vietnam policy.

In this case, party loyalty won out over progressivism and Hatfield agreed to curtail his attacks while the Nixon administration examined its positions.[10]

The Partnership with McGovern

As Hatfield became increasingly frustrated with President Nixon's foreign policy, Wes Michaelson came to work at Hatfield's office as an unpaid intern. Michaelson had met Hatfield at the national Presidential Prayer Breakfast the year before and the two had talked about their shared evangelical faith and their similar views on Vietnam.

Michaelson hailed from a relatively conservative background, but had become concerned about the Vietnam War while taking theology and political science classes at Princeton. After Michaelson finished his time as an intern, the staff members responsible for most of the research and legwork on the Vietnam initiatives left the Hatfield staff and Michaelson moved into a regular staff role as a speech writer and legislative strategist. He soon met other staffers on Capitol Hill who had similar views on Vietnam, and he began collaborating with them on peace initiatives. Some of these were legislative efforts and some were designed to mobilize public concern about the issue.[11]

Hatfield's next Vietnam initiative involved supporting a measure that would have repealed the Gulf of Tonkin resolution, the primary statutory basis for expanding the war. He also cosponsored a resolution authored by Democratic senator Frank Church from the neighboring state of Idaho, calling for the withdrawal of all U.S. troops from Vietnam. While President Nixon had brought some troops home by then, Church and Hatfield calculated it would take at least ten years to get them all home at that rate of withdrawal.

Linking with the efforts of various organizations to generate public concern about the war, Hatfield supported a day of public education on October 15, 1969, in Washington, D.C. He hoped it would spur discussion and reflection without stimulating agitation—a sentiment that reflected the cautious side of his progressivism. (Hatfield regularly refrained from supporting the more strident antiwar groups.) The public education event was peaceful and successful with an estimated 100,000 participants.[12]

As Nixon's first year in office neared an end, Hatfield and other antiwar senators became less and less optimistic that the president would move the country toward peace in Vietnam. Consequently they began developing a piece of legislation that they thought might attract enough votes to pass, and in so doing convince the White House to get more serious about ending the war. George McGovern, Democrat from South Dakota, emerged from these discussions as Hatfield's principal partner. Others active in the discussion were Democrats Alan Cranston of California and Harold Hughes of Iowa, and fellow Republican moderate Charles Goodell of New York. This intentionally bipartisan antiwar coalition was made up of articulate senators highly regarded by their colleagues. Whereas Senator Church's measure a few months before would have immediately withdrawn all troops, the Hatfield-McGovern measure took a more politically prudent approach. It required the United States to withdraw all troops from Cambodia within 30 days, but allowed the administration a full year to get all U.S. soldiers out of Vietnam.[13]

What Hatfield and McGovern could never have done to generate support for their measure, the administration did just days after the bill's introduction—it sent troops into Cambodia to locate North Vietnamese forces. For months the United States had bombed areas along Cambodia's border with Vietnam, but sending in ground troops violated assurances Nixon had given to the government of Cambodia that America would honor Cambodia's attempt to remain neutral. Shortly after Nixon announced this expansion of the war, students at Kent State University in Ohio organized a protest. Frightened National Guard troops began firing on the protestors, killing four of them. The Kent State Massacre, as it came to be called, energized the antiwar movement and put the spotlight on the Hatfield-McGovern amendment as the most immediate opportunity for congressionally initiated change.

Even though the Hatfield-McGovern amendment did not take an extreme approach, Senator Fulbright and fellow members of the Foreign Relations Committee declined to support it because it set a specific date for withdrawing U.S. troops from Vietnam. Nevertheless, in May 1970 Hatfield and McGovern decided to move ahead with the measure, since the administration had begun a military escalation of the conflict. Through the summer of 1970, the Nixon administration

116

urged congressional leaders to delay a vote on the Hatfield-McGovern amendment. Since it's always easier to arrange for a delay in congressional action than to expedite it, the tactics of the White House staff succeeded.

In September, when the measure finally came to a vote, Hatfield's remarks on the Senate floor mirrored points he had made in *Not Quite So Simple*. He emphasized the constitutional role that Congress had neglected—that of giving proper deliberation and consent to war efforts. He assured senators that passing the measure would strengthen the movement toward a negotiated peace, rather than hindering these efforts as opponents had argued.[14]

To the surprise of some and the disappointment of others, 37 senators voted for the Hatfield-McGovern amendment. The measure would have passed if only eight senators had voted differently. McGovern and Hatfield had talked personally with many senators and believed they had persuaded some undecided voters. Because of the relatively strong support for the amendment, McGovern and Hatfield agreed to continue the fight. McGovern, Hatfield, and their allies—Church, Hughes, and Goodell—participated in a television program intended to further mobilize public support for their antiwar efforts. Viewers responded generously to their appeal to help underwrite the costs of the program, and the senators used the surplus to purchase newspaper and radio advertising.[15]

During this time, Hatfield asked Wes Michaelson to go to Vietnam to gather evidence. While there, Michaelson concluded that the American effort to defeat the Vietcong was faltering, the government of South Vietnam had little popular support, and its armies were hopelessly weak.

In 1971 McGovern and Hatfield tried several more times to get enough votes to pass a troop withdrawal measure. Since McGovern's efforts in seeking the Democratic presidential nomination the following year preoccupied him, Democratic senator Lawton Chiles from Florida stepped forward with a measure almost identical to the Hatfield-McGovern text. The Chiles amendment had secured the 50 votes it needed to pass (only 99 senators were then present). As so often happens with close measures, however, the final tally was changed through some arm-twisting before the end of the roll call. Senator John Stennis persuaded Senator B. Everett Jordan, Democrat from North

Carolina and a previous supporter of the Hatfield-McGovern amendment, to change his vote to "no," resulting in the measure's defeat.

During the debate, Hatfield decried the deaths of more than 2,800 American servicemen since the defeat of the resolution the year before. It frustrated him that he and his colleagues had won enough total votes on the various amendments to assure passage, but they never had enough "yes" votes at any one time. In part, this reflected the senators' practice of watching the final count and changing their votes at the last moment to assure defeat, while still hoping to find a way to satisfy their antiwar constituents.[16]

Gaining a National Hearing

An interesting assortment of groups supported Hatfield in these antiwar efforts. He and his staff continued to collaborate with many peace groups in seeking to intensify public opposition to the war, or at least to soften the support Johnson and Nixon had built up. Meanwhile, evangelical Christian groups continued to invite Hatfield to speak, for they admired his articulate expression of personal Christian faith. Before many of these groups, however, Hatfield expressed an impassioned plea for backing the antiwar movement, something many in these audiences would not support.

Hatfield spoke to the Southern Baptist Convention—about as theologically and politically conservative an audience as he could have selected—regarding his puzzlement that President Johnson had said in his 1964 campaign that the war in Indochina was an Asian war and that Asian soldiers should carry it on. Yet over time the government of South Vietnam had become very dependent on the American military for personnel and equipment. Two years later Hatfield spoke to the U.S. Congress on Evangelism. There he laid out many of his antiwar themes and his talk appeared in a number of Christian magazines, but he probably did not win many converts to his position.

Audiences of this type tolerated Hatfield's Vietnam message, in part because they trusted him as an evangelical Christian and as a Republican. But more and more evangelicals began writing to him, telling him they despised his stand on the war and doubted the validity of his Christian testimony. Conservative Oregonians felt no happier with Hatfield in 1971 than when they had voted against him in 1966.

So Hatfield faced decision time, since his campaign plans needed to be in place well before the end of 1971. Since Oregon's primary occurs in May of the election year, credible candidates begin serious campaigning by January.

Vietnam and the Decision to Run Again

The substantial arguments against running for reelection had much to do with Hatfield's unpopular position on Vietnam. In his book *Between a Rock and a Hard Place,* published a few years after the 1972 election, Hatfield recounted his agonizing decision about running again.

He felt tired of *almost* getting enough votes to challenge the president's conduct of the Vietnam War. He felt tired from taking stands against various military programs the White House kept promoting, such as the Anti-Ballistic Missile program and the Supersonic Transport program (with both civilian and military applications). In short, he felt worn out from putting forth so much effort and having so little to show for it.

One factor significantly influenced Hatfield's thinking about the 1972 race: the defeat of his Senate ally in the Vietnam struggle, New York Republican Charles Goodell. In spite of being the incumbent, Goodell lost his seat to Conservative Party candidate, James Buckley, receiving fewer than 25 percent of the votes. White House opposition to Goodell helped to assure his defeat, and Hatfield knew that Nixon's staff considered his own voting record no more palatable than Goodell's had been. In fact, Vice President Spiro Agnew gave speeches that called people like Hatfield "radic-libs." There was a real possibility that the White House staff would strenuously oppose Hatfield's reelection.[17]

But Hatfield also struggled with broader issues in his decision about running again. He did not believe that he should routinely and automatically run for reelection to *any* office, and this was his first chance to decide about staying in the U.S. Senate. He believed that he had to develop his positions on difficult issues like the Vietnam War without basing his decision primarily on its impact on a reelection bid. He said he refused to "make a deal with Mephistopheles" for the sake of political security, and instead he had to be willing to walk away from his position in the Senate. He had enjoyed his teaching and administrative work at Willamette University and considered a return to academia an attractive option if his own decision-making or even the electoral process moved him to make a change.

Every time Hatfield got ready to announce his decision about running for office, he made a trip to Silverton, Oregon, where he had made his first announcement about running for the legislature. Each time he stood up to announce his plans, he said he had come with two speeches in his coat pocket, one saying "No, I won't run" and the other saying "Yes, I will run." While insiders knew which speech he planned to give, this ritual had a serious side to it: He determined to hold lightly the privileges of his office. If he decided not to run, he wanted to be willing to walk away from it all.[18]

Hatfield's movement from discouragement and despair to a renewed commitment to his work in the Senate came about in the autumn of 1971, prior to the traditional announcement event. As noted earlier, when he left Washington for the summer recess, he told Wes Michaelson that if he were making the decision at that time, he would not run again. But by autumn he had begun to think differently about the decision.

On the one hand, he faced a very discouraging political situation. It felt daunting to face a majority of voters still unhappy with his outspoken leadership against the Vietnam War. But characteristically, his decision to run again became a spiritual process more than a political one. While taking long walks on the Oregon beach, he felt drawn back to his original calling to public office. He later spoke of his time in Oregon as an exercise in renewing his "vision of prophetic witness, faithfulness, and servanthood."[19]

Despite his decision to stay in politics, Hatfield faced a real battle for reelection. His constituents continued to write to him, accusing him of abandoning his faith by frequently disagreeing with President Nixon. They quoted Romans 13 in the New Testament, which speaks of God placing heads of state in their positions. This, they said, required Christians to support Richard Nixon if they intended to remain faithful to the Bible's teaching. Some even used the word *treason* to describe Hatfield's role in the antiwar movement. Even his pastor in Oregon sharply criticized him. And state polls confirmed his unpopularity, just as they had in 1966. While Hatfield never had a high view

STAND ALONE OR COME HOME

of opinion polls, it discouraged him to hear that the polls said Governor McCall could have defeated him in the Republican primary and that one of Oregon's House members, Democrat Edith Green, could defeat him in the general election. So much for the presumed advantage of incumbency![20]

Hatfield's visibility in national politics in some ways became a liability in Oregon. Only four years earlier at the Republican convention some had thought Hatfield might be selected as Nixon's running mate.[21] Some Oregonians felt proud of Hatfield's growing national following, but others equated his broader political activity with neglecting the needs of the state. Moreover, during his first term Hatfield had spoken frequently outside of Oregon. First he had given speeches supporting Nixon's candidacy, then he gave many speeches against the Vietnam War—speeches to numerous colleges and universities and regular sermons and messages at Christian gatherings. These activities worried Hatfield's campaign volunteers in Oregon, for they heard many people grumbling that the senator was neglecting the state.

But as the 1972 campaign got underway, the decisions of other potential candidates improved Hatfield's situation dramatically. Both Governor McCall and Congresswoman Green decided not to enter the race. Then former U.S. senator Morse entered the race. Morse had lost his seat to the much younger Republican, Robert Packwood, in 1968 and felt eager to return to Congress. But on Vietnam and a number of other issues, Morse's views did not differ substantially from Hatfield's, and he could not legitimately criticize Hatfield's views on the war.

Alongside Morse's maverick tendencies, Hatfield appeared to be more consistent and principled. When the editors of *The Oregonian* gave Hatfield their reluctant endorsement, they characterized Hatfield as the lesser of two evils. At the time *The Oregonian* held mostly conservative views and its editors didn't like Hatfield's stand on the war. But age was an issue for the newspaper, since Hatfield was fifty and Morse was seventy-two. So the newspaper backed Hatfield.

Once election officials finished the count, Hatfield had kept his winning record intact. While he had won no landslide by garnering 53.7 percent of the total votes, he felt encouraged to have improved two points over his showing in the election six years earlier.[22]

The Beginning of the End of the War

After the election the war seemed to be moving into its final stages. The Nixon administration appeared to have little choice but to begin considering an exit strategy. In January 1973, Nixon announced the suspension of U.S. offensive action in Vietnam. The signing of the Paris Peace Accords shortly after that brought an eventual halt to the U.S. role in the war.

As the war came to an end, Hatfield believed a related issue deserved attention. Hatfield had regularly spoken of the draft as a factor in the weakness of the U.S. military effort. He considered many of the draftees poorly trained and believed their short terms of service hindered their effectiveness. He reflected on his own eagerness to fight in World War II, a conflict he and most Americans fully supported, but he noted that Vietnam draftees came heavily from lower-income population groups and they felt they were unduly bearing the human costs of the war. Those with the means to attend universities and graduate schools tended to receive student deferments, so students from middle- and upper-income families did not generally serve in Vietnam. And for most of the war, eighteen- to twenty-year-olds were not yet old enough to vote. They could be ordered into battle, but had no voice in selecting those who determined their fate.[23]

It is clear, therefore, that Hatfield's opposition to the draft came about largely because of his opposition to the Vietnam War. He opposed this particular war, not all war, and he couldn't bear the thought of sending more young men into a conflict he considered so deeply wrong. He introduced bills to repeal the draft in 1967, in 1969, and in 1970, none of which passed. But after Senator Mike Gravel's extended filibuster in 1971 against extending the draft, President Nixon agreed with congressional leaders to allow conscription to expire in 1973. Seven years later, Congress reinstated the requirement that young men register with the Selective Service System to speed up activation of the draft in a national emergency, but this system has not led to the renewal of conscription.

As the Vietnam peace process concluded, Hatfield took still more political risks by speaking out for amnesty for draft evaders, draft resisters, and principled deserters. In a coauthored book published in

1973, Hatfield articulated the middle ground in a "point/counter point" set of arguments. In *Amnesty? The Unsettled Question of Vietnam*, he laid out the case for amnesty for those who had refused service in Vietnam. He based his argument on history, pointing out that amnesty had been granted after past U.S. wars.

Hatfield asserted that most Americans had come to recognize the error of the nation's involvement in Indochina and that this recognition should lead to a spirit of forgiveness of (or at least tolerance for) those who, for reasons of conscience, had refused to participate in the war. He argued for a prompt amnesty process for those clearly motivated by genuine conscientious objection to the Vietnam War. He also proposed the creation of amnesty appeal councils to consider the specifics of individual cases. He hoped that these actions might "build the climate for a spirit of reconciliation to reign, ending the war that has raged not only beyond our land, but within it."[24]

A final stage of Hatfield's involvement in Vietnam issues came from his concern over prisoners of war (POWs) and personnel declared missing in action. Hatfield learned that the Vietnamese might still be holding some American civilians, in particular some missionaries who had been working in Vietnam. Hoping he might be able to relieve the suffering of families who did not know the fate of their loved ones, he did what he could within the Appropriations Committee to provide adequate funding for the U.S. investigation into these reports. After the North Vietnamese released some prisoners to prominent peace activists, Hatfield thought he would try to negotiate for the release of others.

To pursue the POW issue, Hatfield sent two of his key staff members, Wes Michaelson and Gerry Frank, to Paris to a meeting arranged by a Quaker group to explore prospects for locating and returning U.S. prisoners. No releases occurred as a result of this contact, but the discussions in Paris helped the peace dialogue to progress. As the hope of finding POWs began to fade, Hatfield supported efforts to look for the remains of those killed in action. These and future efforts did not yield much, but Hatfield considered it both right and necessary to pursue these inquiries.[25]

On to Other Issues

For most of the first decade of Hatfield's Senate career, Vietnam remained his defining issue. But as the United States prepared to extract itself from Southeast Asia, it became possible for this progressive evangelical to attend to a number of other global needs that compelled him.

10

GLOBAL HUNGER AND POVERTY

In his book, *God's Politics,* Jim Wallis tells of being part of a group of seminary students who located many Bible passages dealing with poverty, injustice, and oppression. One member of the group found an old Bible and cut out all the verses and passages they found on these subjects. Instead of a "holy Bible" in the usual sense of the phrase, they had created a Bible full of holes, lacking in much of the content of the faith.[1]

Wallis claims that many evangelical conservatives have a blind spot regarding the gospel's focus on ministering to those in need. If anything, this problem was even more acute during Hatfield's early Senate career than it is today.

His New Cause—The Poor of the World

Two years into his first term in the Senate, Mark Hatfield gave the closing prayer at the Presidential Prayer Breakfast in Washington. He prayed that the president and other national leaders would succeed in their quest for peace. Yet instead of identifying the nation's enemies as communists and totalitarians, he asserted that the real enemies were disease, hunger, and poverty.

Later that year, Hatfield spoke in a religious service in the Pentagon and further developed this thought. "As long as there is deprivation, suffering, alienation, self-seeking, and exploitation there is no real peace," Hatfield said. "Peace can come only when needs—physical and spiritual—are fulfilled."

Hatfield then discussed the Hebrew term for peace—*shalom*—which brings together the concepts of the well-being of individuals and harmony among nations. He urged his audience of military leaders to bind up the wounds of the world's suffering people and to fill their empty stomachs. This, he said, would be the greatest contribution they could make to global peace.[2]

Senator Hatfield's emphasis on the needs of the poor came directly from his Christian worldview. "It has become increasingly obvious to me that Christians reaching out in deed as well as word to touch the lives of the poor, the oppressed, the lonely, and the frightened, are the only expression in the flesh of the living Christ that many people are going to know," Hatfield wrote.[3]

Hatfield frequently cited scriptural passages such as Matthew 25, which declares that the followers of Christ will be judged on the basis of their treatment of the hungry, the thirsty, the sick, those in need of clothes, and those in prison. And he asserted that the "Great Commission" to preach the gospel to the spiritually lost included a mandate to respond to the needs of the world's poor. In a speech to the Southern Baptist Convention in 1967—a group devoting a great deal of energy to global evangelism—Hatfield declared that too often the compassionate response to human need went missing from Christian world evangelism.[4]

Hatfield's emphasis on responding to the needs of the world's poor also can be traced to one of his greatest political heroes, Herbert Hoover. Hatfield wrote his master's degree thesis at Stanford University on Hoover and continued throughout his political career to speak of Hoover's success in directing European relief efforts after World War I. By working on the supply side to increase U.S. agricultural production and also on the logistics of shipping food to Europe, Hoover succeeding in quadrupling U.S. food exports by 1918. Hatfield represented Oregon, a state with considerable capacity for wheat production, and felt that it would enhance the agricultural economy to once more increase shipments of food to the hungry.[5]

Seeing Global Poverty Firsthand

Hatfield's concern for the world's needy also came from his firsthand experiences in seeing great need. Just as visiting postwar Japan and

Indochina had reinforced his growing concern about the inadequacy of military solutions to the world's problems, so Hatfield's close contact with starving people forever changed him.

In Hiroshima he saw not only the devastation caused by the first atomic weapon, but he also saw many ravenous children and adults who had lost all sources of food and physical well-being. In a brief stop in Indochina, he saw even more hunger, caused not by war but (in Hatfield's judgment) from the oppression of the French. Many times his thoughts turned back to these experiences in Asia as he reflected on the evils of war and the broader problems of poverty and oppression.[6]

Another firsthand exposure to poverty with an equally lasting impression was a trip to Calcutta, India. Hatfield and his family went there to visit Mother Teresa—founder of the Missionaries of Charity order. Starting with the organization's orphanage, then spending time at the home for the dying, and ending with the order's work among the lepers, the Hatfields felt deeply moved. As the senator's family got ready to leave, they encountered a young mother outside the gates of the order's compound. She was waiting for a chance to give her dying baby to Mother Teresa, desperately hoping that the child's life might be spared. This act symbolized for Hatfield the desperation of the poor, who saw no other hope for the survival of their children than to give them away.

The visit to Calcutta became what Hatfield later called, "one of the greatest highlights of my life." Several years later he invited Mother Teresa to speak to his staff in Washington. One staff member recalls Mother Teresa challenging this group of young professionals to give everything they had to the poor, which she said was what Jesus had done.[7]

A Concern Reinforced

As Senator Hatfield began shifting his focus from the Vietnam War to the issue of global hunger, he found this concern reinforced by the citizens of Oregon. At one point he received some letters written by elementary school students in Yamhill, Oregon, a small agricultural community about an hour west of Portland. One letter spoke of having seen photographs of starving children in the *Weekly Reader* paper at school. The child requested that Hatfield buy cattle from farmers and give the meat to the poor. Another child spoke of the wrongness of letting the world's hungry die. "If we were them they would send food to us. Why don't you do something?"[8]

Hatfield knew it was easier to talk about the needy than to mobilize the government's resources to respond to these needs. Republicans often railed against exorbitant government outlays for "lazy" welfare recipients—Hatfield himself had criticized elements of the welfare system—but his comments did not echo the conservative litany of attacks. Hatfield's main emphasis was on the demeaning aspects of the public assistance programs that caused recipients to lose their dignity, self-respect, and their capacity to contribute to society.[9]

Hatfield often spoke to churches and religious organizations about the welfare system, reminding them that their faith compelled them to help the needy of their communities, instead of merely complain about welfare programs. He called on the delegates to the Southern Baptist Convention in 1967 to stop attacking the government's wasteful spending on human assistance programs and to begin doing something about the needy in their communities. He claimed there were about a million Americans at that time whose physical condition prevented them from earning a livelihood. The math was simple, he said. If each of the 300,000 churches in the United States helped just three of the neediest residents of their communities, government welfare programs would no longer be needed. He wanted people to see the inconsistency of criticizing government waste when they did very little to meet the needs that welfare programs addressed.[10]

Hatfield also proposed the unconventional idea of decentralizing political power and giving much of the responsibility to neighborhood and community governments. His idea for "neighborhood government" would have offered a tax credit for donating up to 80 percent of one's federal tax obligations to neighborhood organizations. With these resources, the neighborhood governments could set about to meet most local needs, including public assistance, law enforcement, and public health services. Instead of sending tax revenues to Washington and then back, Hatfield reasoned, taxes kept at the local level with maximum local input about their use would constitute the ultimate in modern democracy.

Grounded in a Republican distrust for big government and an almost libertarian desire to streamline government to the basics, Hatfield saw the neighborhood government proposal as a practical way to meet the needs of the poor and the working classes. He cited prototypes in the "Sto-Rox" community near Pittsburgh and the Adams Morgan neighborhood association of Washington, D.C. While he regularly introduced legislation on this type of structural change, he found little support on Capitol Hill.[11]

More in the mainstream of American political progressivism was Hatfield's unending call for more frugality in military spending and greater generosity in meeting human needs both inside and outside the country. In a 1970 speech he looked ahead to the end of the Vietnam War and called for shifting resources from the military to the needs of the poor. He called on his mostly conservative audience to stifle their fears of big government, socialism, and the welfare state to support a massive shift from wartime spending to peacetime generosity in meeting human need. He predicted that people would want their taxes cut after the war and urged the creation of what would later be called a "peace dividend." He argued not merely that it was morally right to provide for the needy, but that a failure to generously give to the poor of the world would contribute to a future uprising of the world's poor.[12]

Ombudsman Hatfield

Senator Hatfield also expressed his compassion by investigating complaints and finding answers when constituents encountered problems with government services. He and his staff functioned as something of an *ombudsman*—a term borrowed from European politics. Some states had created ombudsman positions—positions for people who investigate complaints and work toward fair settlements—but no such thing exists at the federal level.

In his preface to an edition of William Wilberforce's book about Christian faithfulness, Hatfield pointed to the need for compassionate intervention on behalf of the needs of people frustrated by bureaucratic confusion and delays. He spoke of the priority he gave to the complaints and inquiries he daily received from Oregonians trying to get their rightful Social Security benefits, veterans benefits, and other federal benefits.

Hatfield assigned several staff people in his Washington and Oregon offices to help individuals get the benefits they deserved. While most of this work required written inquiries, the staff knew that in special situations Hatfield would call the head of the agency to request an investigation. Grateful constituents often spread the word about the help they had received, so this kind of assistance did generate a political payoff. But Hatfield saw this ombudsman work as a key part of his public service, not just good politics.[13]

A Surprising Choice?

As Hatfield began his second term in the Senate, his choice to serve on the Appropriations Committee surprised many. Since he had gained national recognition as a vocal critic of the Vietnam War, they expected him to seek a place on the Foreign Relations Committee; indeed, some key staff members hoped he would do just that.

But Hatfield knew the limitations of serving on the Foreign Relations Committee. While that committee regularly makes headlines with its hearings on major global issues, often it can do very little to influence the global policies of the White House. Most presidents, after all, prefer to develop and execute foreign policy with limited intrusions from Congress.

Hatfield also knew that constituents might become concerned about his priorities if he appeared more interested in global issues than in local issues. This perception, in fact, became a factor in the later defeat of his colleague from the neighboring state of Idaho, Senator Frank Church, who held the chairmanship of the Foreign Relations Committee when he lost a reelection bid in 1980.

As a member of the Appropriations Committee, Hatfield knew he could have *some* influence over almost *any* issue, and a great deal of clout on some concerns. He understood that local projects—such as shipping facilities in coastal port districts—had important regional and national benefits, and his recent campaign had reminded him of the importance of keeping voters happy. Regarding the broader national issues such as health care, he considered service on the Appropriations Committee as an opportunity to do a great deal of good on behalf of human needs.

In his memoirs, Hatfield recalled an instance in which being on the Appropriations Committee gave him opportunity to provide funds for seeking a cure for an obscure disease. Some ailments, called "orphan diseases," had no registry of victims, no database of specialists treating the diseases, and no roster of groups urging greater attention to the disorder. One day a young man who had one of these diseases—epidermolysis bullosa (EB)—came to his office. A staff member talked with the young man and felt moved by the boy's courage despite intense physical suffering. Hatfield met the boy and immediately invited him to testify before an appropriation subcommittee that dealt with the year's requests for health research. The boy's moving testimony had the desired effect. The bill went forward with funds in it to help victims of the disease. The opportunity to advocate for increased funding to meet human needs was certainly one of the benefits of being on the Appropriations Committee.[14]

The World Food Conference

While Hatfield gained influence and expertise in the appropriations process, he continued to maintain his interest in global issues. The pending U.S. withdrawal from Vietnam opened the way for him to look at human needs more broadly.

In the early 1970s famine conditions in Bangladesh (formerly East Pakistan) began to grip the world's attention. At the same time food shortages continued to cause suffering in various parts of Africa. In November 1974, the U.N.'s Food and Agriculture Organization convened a large gathering in Rome for policy makers and agricultural experts, a conference often called the World Food Summit. Senator Hatfield chose to join the American delegation, believing that the conference could deepen his understanding of the issues. He had actively supported such Christian humanitarian groups as World Vision and wanted to determine if the U.S. government could take steps to prevent the needless deaths of the millions around the world. He asked Wes Michaelson, the staff person who had the greatest influence on his progressive evangelical values, to accompany him.

Hatfield listened as experts presented gloomy predictions of modest increases in food production, dramatic increases in population, more frequent weather patterns detrimental to crop production, the increasing costs of sustaining the production gains made during the "Green Revolution," and major deficits in food supplies. But Hatfield interpreted the information differently from some of the presenters and delegates.

According to conventional wisdom, there were solutions available for rural development, such as disseminating "Green Revolution" technology, achieving zero population growth, and creating a world food bank. But Hatfield saw a more fundamental and obvious solution: reducing consumption among the affluent residents of industrialized "First-World" countries. He reasoned this action would free up resources to solve the problem of global hunger, which in his opinion was poverty, not merely inadequate production. The hungry simply didn't have the resources to buy food, even when it became available within their own countries.[15]

Not only did Hatfield believe that some presenters at the conference missed the point, he considered some members of the U.S. delegation seriously misguided. Secretary of Agriculture Earl Butz headed the American delegation and defended the status quo in world food distribution, a system intended (in Hatfield's view) primarily to shore up prices for American farm products. Butz insisted that the conference should look at long-range production issues, not deal with short-term starvation problems.

Hatfield compared Butz's approach to "urging firemen to ignore blazing cities in favor of discussions about future fire prevention."[16] Hatfield also felt appalled at some statements made by Secretary of State Henry Kissinger, who declared at the conference that in another decade, no child in the world would need to go to bed hungry. Hatfield supported the goal, but did not believe the leading voices at the conference had any credible plans to reach the goal. The conference adopted a statement affirming the principle that everyone in the world had the right to be free from hunger, but acknowledged that affirming that right would do little to provide sufficient food resources for the very poor.

Hatfield later said that responding to the world's nutritional needs must begin with something more basic than increasing production in the developed world. He insisted that global hunger could not be addressed without land reform. Too few people in the developing world had access to land, he declared, since local elites and foreign landowners controlled much of the most productive land. Effective land reform, he said, had to create parcels of land small enough for labor-intensive and low-input farming.

Hatfield recalled talking with a delegate to the Rome conference from Tanzania, who criticized the call for agricultural mechanization. "Why bring in tractors and displace farm workers?" asked the African. Hatfield agreed and also asserted that land parcels needed to be large enough to support the extended families typical of people in the Global South. Farmers needed resources to increase their production, and Hatfield proposed that such resources be channeled through farm cooperatives, entities that in turn would organize marketing processes to negotiate fair prices for the farmers.[17]

Reforms in Food Aid

Hatfield returned from the World Food Conference knowing that land reform would be a slow and difficult process. So he turned instead to legislation that would increase the flow of U.S. farm products to the needy of the world.

It seemed logical to Hatfield to make improvements in the primary existing channel of food aid, the Agricultural Trade Development and Assistance Act of 1954, commonly called the "P.L. [Public Law] 480" or the Food for Peace program. To most observers, the P.L. 480 program that dealt with U.S. farm surpluses by shipping food to needy areas where prices wouldn't fall—since the needy recipients had no money to buy the food anyway—seemed like a laudable effort.

But in reality, the P.L. 480 program had many flaws. Countries receiving the food under Title I of the program were obliged to pay for it later, which was out of the question for most of the very poor countries. Title II authorized giving food to needy countries, but Hatfield knew that problems existed with the allocations of these gifts. The volume of Title II food had steadily declined and President Ford and his advisors refused to consider increasing it. More significantly, the food aid went primarily to U.S. allies in strategic areas, principally Southeast Asia. To make matters worse, a good bit of the "food aid" consisted of non-edible products such as tobacco and cotton. So it seemed obvious to Hatfield that the program had become principally an outlet for excess U.S. production, not a channel for global compassion.

One might have expected that a growing awareness of world hunger generated by the Rome conference and the subsequent news coverage of droughts and starvation around the world would have assured support for Hatfield's legislation to reform the P.L. 480 program. Not so. He suffered a quick defeat when he attempted to exclude non-food items, such as tobacco and cotton. Members of Congress from states growing those crops historically worked together to protect the outlets for their surplus commodities, and they quickly marshaled their strength to eliminate the non-food exclusion.

Also, those who wanted to protect the flow of food to strategic allies successfully limited that feature of the bill to a 30-percent cap on aid to non-needy nations. Yet political achievements generally involve compromise, and Hatfield—with the notable support of Democratic Senator Hubert Humphrey—got the reform bill passed, even though it lacked provisions he considered important. He made a point of meeting with President Gerald Ford, urging that the president sign the bill into law over the objections of Secretary Kissinger. The struggle didn't end there, however. Later Hatfield had to take the floor of the Senate to call Secretary Kissinger to account for ignoring the 30-percent cap while giving food aid to South Vietnam, Chile, and South Korea.[18]

After achieving some success in reforming the P.L. 480 program, Hatfield proposed a much more aggressive program of mobilizing U.S. agriculture to produce and ship food where it was most needed. He based this proposition on the success stories from Herbert Hoover in mobilizing American farmers to provide relief to the hungry in Europe after World War I. President Wilson appointed Hoover as U.S. food administrator in 1917 with a mandate to stimulate increased U.S. farm production and to organize the shipment of the food to starving war victims. The results spoke for themselves, Hatfield often reminded people. U.S. food exports went from just over 5 million tons in 1917 to 20 million tons two years later.[19]

Hatfield's proposal to revive the Hoover program included the idea of appointing a "food czar" with substantial authority, like later proposals for a U.S. "drug czar." Hatfield did not generally favor the proliferation of new federal agencies and officials, but his bill would have established an Office of Food Administration to coordinate and mobilize efforts to accelerate U.S. farm production and export. The head of the office would have held cabinet rank and the political clout to be able to insist on cooperation from the appropriate agencies—the State Department and its foreign aid branch, the U.S. Agency for International Development, as well as the Department of Agriculture. Secretaries Kissinger and Butz had no desire to upset the status quo in this way, however, nor did they want their authority restricted. So they and their White House allies sent word to Capitol Hill that this legislation should not go forward. And it did not.[20]

A Call for Fasting and Prayer

With little to show for his legislative initiatives regarding the global hunger problem, Hatfield took some symbolic steps that would at least help educate the American public about the crisis. In December 1973, just before the congressional recess for the holidays, he took the Senate floor with a resolution that drew on Abraham Lincoln's call for a national day of humiliation, prayer, and fasting in the midst of the horrible suffering of the Civil War.

Hatfield updated the language and added a section on the neglect of human needs abroad. He said the American people had "failed to respond, personally and collectively, with sacrifice and uncompromised commitment to the unmet needs of our fellow men, both at home and abroad."[21] Hatfield felt pleased and a little surprised when the Senate majority leader, Mike Mansfield, exercised his authority as floor leader to call for the immediate consideration of the Hatfield resolution. It passed without objection. Mansfield knew that few senators would complain about a resolution that required the government to do nothing and would cost nothing in taxpayer funds. But the measure had no champion in the House and it never made it out of the House Judiciary Committee.

A similar fate awaited Hatfield's "Thanksgiving Resolution," which he introduced in the Senate after returning from the World Food Conference. Based on the assumption that Americans needed to think seriously about world hunger, Hatfield's resolution called for a renewed focus on world hunger between the Thanksgiving holidays in 1974 and 1975. It called on Americans to share from their bounty by eating less and by giving from their savings to provide food for the hungry. It asked that this special observance culminate in a national day of fasting on the Monday before Thanksgiving 1975. Again, Hatfield's resolution passed the Senate but died in the House.[22]

The Coffee Boycott

Disappointed by the results of his efforts regarding global human needs, Hatfield seized an opportunity to use the legislative process to respond to an instance of political oppression. Its scale was much narrower than what Hatfield had been pouring energy into, but it did address the issues of human suffering and it was successful.

An Anglican clergyman named Bishop Festo Kivengere came to see Hatfield to tell him about the problems in his native land of Uganda, from which he was then in exile. A former British colony, Uganda had a many natural resources and had achieved independence without the "Mau Mau" type of violence suffered by neighboring Kenya. Uganda's violent experiences came after independence when Idi Amin, a soldier with almost no education—but a good bit of skill and ambition—successfully organized a military coup and named himself Uganda's president in 1971.

Senator Hatfield was touched by Bishop Kivengere's stories of the awful violence in Uganda. Amin's agents of murder had killed Kivengere's superior in the church, the Anglican archbishop Janani Luwum. With great difficulty, Kivengere had escaped to exile in the United States where he was living when Hatfield heard his plea for help. The bishop later told his story in a remarkably titled booklet, *I Love Idi Amin*.[23]

The United States had closed its embassy in Uganda in 1976, almost eliminating the already meager channels of communication between the two governments. How could a senator with only a little seniority do much about a brutal dictator in a country where the United States had no strategic interests? Oddly enough, the answer that Hatfield and Kivengere discussed involved food—or at least a beverage.

A considerable amount of Uganda's foreign exchange came from the export of coffee. That revenue had been funding Amin's access to weapons and ammunition that were so necessary to sustain his regime. Even before the present fascination with gourmet coffees, Proctor and Gamble and other American businesses had begun importing significant amounts of Ugandan coffee for U.S. consumers.

So to challenge Amin's violent regime, Hatfield fashioned a bill to ban further imports of Ugandan coffee. While Hatfield generally favored free trade, he didn't mind proposing a modest restriction on trade in order to try to stop a maniacal dictator. This time Hatfield found an ally in the Senate in Lowell Weicker of Connecticut, a progressive Republican colleague. Hearings on the measure attracted considerable attention and to the surprise of some, the measure passed both houses of Congress. At the signing ceremony, President Carter pointed out to Senator Hatfield that he had signed the bill against the advice of State Department and White House officials. Yet the counsel Carter received from church leaders and Carter's commitment to global human rights prompted him to override the advice of his senior officials.

The coffee boycott was a modest step, but in short order Ugandan exiles received help from the Tanzanian army to force Amin to flee the country. When Amin surrendered power and left the country— never to return to power—Hatfield and his staff celebrated it as a victory.[24]

Stewards of Justice

At the end of a chapter on world hunger in his book *Between a Rock and a Hard Place,* Hatfield incorporates his concern for the needy of the world in a statement that captures a number of his related values:

> What is our country, if not our land and our bountiful resources of all kinds, and above all, the people? So let us love the land, and preserve it as an environment which nurtures the whole life of our people. Let us be stewards of justice over our resources, sharing and utilizing them for the sake of all humanity. And let all of us be inspired to a relevant and sacrificial commitment of our lives to the destiny of those who are poor, hungry, and oppressed. Then shall we discover true greatness, even that shown to us by the One who came to serve, and emptied himself, washing the feet of others.[25]

This statement directly connects Hatfield's involvement with global human needs to his concerns for the land and the environment. What responsibility do believers in Christ have to wisely steward God's creation? Hatfield's progressive politics made no attempt to avoid that question.

11

CONCERN FOR GOD'S CREATION

Mark Hatfield became part of an increasing sensitivity among evangelicals about the wise use of God's created order. Evangelicals typically emphasize the Genesis account of creation and argue against ideas of evolution, which often leave God out of the views about the earth. Some Christians believe that managing the world's resources means the freedom to use those resources without restraint, since they come from God's abundance. But the new evangelical environmentalists, including Mark Hatfield, turned back to the biblical concept of *stewardship*, defining it as the careful, responsible use and management of what God has provided.[1]

Conservation of the Created Order

Senator Hatfield framed his initial ideas about the created order around the concept of conservation, and especially applied this to the wise management of the thousands of acres of forests in the Northwest. Most Oregon politicians have understood the importance of wood products in the state's economy. While the forest-products industry was on the decline during Hatfield's later years in office, for most of his time in the Senate it was the principal arena for conflicting views of the earth's care.

Hatfield credited the forester Gifford Pinchot with pioneering a way of managing forests to make them both productive and sustainable. Pinchot did his undergraduate work at Yale College and studied forestry at the graduate level in France. He later helped establish Yale's School of Forestry and went on to become the first head of the U.S. Forest Service.

Like Pinchot, Hatfield had an understanding of forest management that insisted the forests' beauty could be guarded while perpetually harvesting and replenishing the timber. Pinchot's moderate views on conservation contrasted with those of people like John Muir, who wanted to completely ban the commercial use of forests. But Pinchot also resisted the anti-conservation goals of some members of Congress who agreed with the lumber companies that the abundance of forest resources rendered conservation measures unnecessary.[2]

Hatfield grew up surrounded by beautiful forests, which sheltered wildlife and provided many recreational opportunities, and this personal background informed his understanding of environmental stewardship. After moving his family to Washington, D.C., he treasured even more the occasional opportunities he had to spend time in his native Oregon, both on constituent-focused trips and on vacations. In particular he enjoyed visiting a place near the Yaquina Head lighthouse on the central Oregon coast near Newport. There he sometimes made his way to a particular stump surrounded by evergreen vegetation. This place became something like a sanctuary and place of meditation and retreat, shaping his insights into the importance of guarding the beauty of the created world.[3]

Hatfield recognized the vastness of the concept of stewardship. He could revel in the beauty of the natural world and speak of the importance to the human spirit of having the space to pursue personal renewal. But Hatfield grew up in the town of Dallas, Oregon, which, like many other Oregon communities along the foothills of the Coast Range and the Cascades, depended on the forest-products industry as well as on agriculture for its livelihood. He knew that one person's sense of awe at the beauty of old-growth forests needed to be respected, as did another's convictions that the forests were an essential source of jobs and economic stability in states like Oregon. And he saw every life stage of a forest as beautiful and precious, not merely its old-growth stage. New plantings of trees after harvest, for example, provide attractive habitats for wildlife and generate clean water and air.

As an Oregonian, Hatfield understood the ideas of conservation and stewardship of the state's major public resources, especially the publicly owned forests that covered almost half the state. But he also considered the many rivers and streams of the state as a very important part of the created order and a treasured public resource. He understood the difficulty of balancing the competing uses of the waterways for shipping, for the nourishment of fish, for agricultural irrigation, for municipal water, and for recreation.

Hatfield felt grateful for the success of early conservation efforts. The establishment of Yellowstone National Park in 1872 inspired efforts in 1902 to create the first national park in Oregon, at Crater Lake. He determined to do what he could to see that Congress gave federal protection to some areas that were geographically unique and to other areas that were historically important. Hatfield successfully supported the creation of the Oregon Dunes National Recreation Area, a project that Richard Neuberger had initiated while serving as one of Oregon's U.S. senators.

Hatfield knew that no matter how many areas received such recognition and protection, the greater challenge came in being good stewards of the millions of acres of forestland that did not have a recognized geological or historic uniqueness. That challenge became an opportunity throughout Hatfield's career.

The Theology of Stewardship

Hatfield's Christian values lay at the core of his understanding of the wise use of natural resources. These values link him to the more recent attention given to the environment by evangelical progressives.

Hatfield looked to the Bible's creation account for an ethic of wise use, standing between the extremes of exploitation and total preservation. He contrasted his own position with those who emphasized preservation and who implied that the natural order was too fragile to be tampered with and used. He turned instead to the Genesis account in the Bible for his Christian values of stewardship.

In his book *Between a Rock and a Hard Place,* Hatfield expresses that he deplores the unfortunate influence of the English words used in the King James Version to translate Genesis 1:26-28, in which God directed that humans should have *dominion* over the earth and should *subdue* it. In Hatfield's opinion, humans had proven only too willing to exercise dominion, but had not paid enough attention to God's commands to Adam and Eve to "take care of" the created world. He believed that while the idea of dominion led to the practice of reckless exploitation and to sacred property rights, the concept of stewardship fit more appropriately with the creation account in Genesis.[4]

CONCERN FOR GOD'S CREATION

Central to the Christian idea of stewardship is an awareness of God's ownership of everything on earth, in a much more fundamental sense than the kind of ownership conveyed by land titles. Scripture overflows with assertions such as that found in Psalm 24:1: "The earth is the Lord's, and everything in it, the world, and all who live in it." Since Hatfield recognized God as the Creator, he viewed human occupancy and management of the land as provisional and temporary. Humans are ultimately accountable to God, who expects us to use natural resources carefully and to assure that these resources continue to be available to future generations. This Old Testament teaching on stewardship carries over into the New Testament, especially in Jesus' frequent use of the word *steward* to describe the one in charge of a resource, the person responsible for its productivity and continuity.[5]

Worshiping the Creator, Not the Creation

Hatfield saw the natural world as created evidence of divine power, not as something sacred and divine in itself. His view stood in opposition to that of some in the environmental movement who viewed stands of old-growth timber (and the endangered species that lived there) as sacred. Hatfield considered these natural resources both important and special, but shied away from calling them sacred, since such a practice seemed almost pantheistic to him. He wanted to worship the Creator, not the creation. While he could admire a majestic Douglas fir tree, he had no interest in worshiping it.

Still, he refused to write off the "tree huggers" who worked so hard to protect the forests. He could applaud their conservation efforts while declining their invitations to hug a tree; he did not consider trees another form of divinity. Hatfield summed up his stewardship views after once again visiting his favorite tree stump on Yaquina Head:

> If we are to allow God's Spirit to renew the face of the earth, the Body of Christ must witness with peculiar clarity and power to the truth that we are not the owners of creation, but rather its stewards, entrusted with its temporary use. We each must live and act in ways that demonstrate loving stewardship of the whole of creation for all of humanity. In so doing, we must fashion those environments, in our cities and in the country, which truly nurture the whole person, and his or her relationship to creation. The phrase describ-

ing followers of Christ as "salt of the earth" has greater material significance than we may realize.[6]

Governor Hatfield and Environmental Issues

Hatfield's keen interest in the environment predated his Senate years. While serving as Oregon governor, Hatfield worked on environmental protection in a number of ways.

The Willamette River, which drains much of western Oregon, had become a convenient dumping place for industries such as paper mills. The city of Portland also had allowed too much dumping of untreated municipal waste into the river, hoping the sewage would float out to the ocean unnoticed. Hatfield pressured the city of Portland to put an end to the pollution, and ultimately, federal water-quality legislation and regulation put an end to the dumping of industrial and municipal waste in the Willamette.

Hatfield also got involved in the monitoring of offshore oil exploration to assure that the exploration process and any actual drilling for oil would not harm the ocean waters. As it turned out, Oregon coastal waters did not harbor viable petroleum supplies comparable to those off the coast of California.[7]

Environmental problems often do not confine themselves to state boundaries, and as a senator, Hatfield began to find greater opportunities to develop and implement his principles of stewardship. For some time Hatfield had been trying to resolve a dispute over the transfer of 8,000 acres of public land that had been promised to Oregon when it became a state in 1859. A century later, Oregon still did not hold title to the land. Hatfield became frustrated with the excuses federal officials gave him for not resolving the matter. Hatfield selected the Senate Interior Committee as one of his first committee assignments, primarily because of its responsibility for major decisions on federal lands.

One day Secretary of the Interior Stewart Udall appeared before the committee seeking support for land transfers to make possible a new national park in northern California. Secretary Udall, who had not acted on the Oregon transfer request while Hatfield served as governor, soon discovered he had to pay attention to this new committee member. Hatfield asserted that if land transfers could be completed to create a new park in California, then surely an obligation more than 100 years in arrears could be fulfilled. Secretary Udall understood Hatfield's point and his department went ahead with both transfer processes.[8]

Stewardship of the Forests

Over time, managing federal timberlands became increasingly central to Hatfield's political agenda. And this agenda presented him with an opportunity to apply his ethics of stewardship to the thorny disputes regarding these resources.

While serving in state government, Hatfield had experienced the polarization between those in the timber industry and environmentalists. At times he became impatient with those who seemed to oppose all timber harvests from public lands; sometimes he called them "lock-up preservationists." He nevertheless thought the forest-products industry had come a long way from the early days when timber harvests took place with little or no regulation.

In the late-19th and early-20th centuries, old-growth forests provided a seemingly endless supply of lumber, so logging companies felt little pressure to replenish the hills and valleys from which they cut trees, whether on private or public land. But as supplies of these great forests dwindled, the private landowners began to realize they must replant what they had harvested. Forestry departments at land-grant universities such as Oregon State College (later University) applied scientific research to the process of growing healthy seedlings for reforestation. And these universities worked on measures for controlling diseases and pests that hindered forest growth.

The federal government and states with forest resources collaborated to adopt new practices of forest management so new stocks of trees would grow up to replace those harvested. And when disastrous fires decimated public and private forestland in Oregon's Coast Range in the 1930s and 1940s, public agencies mobilized thousands of private citizens to replant the burned acreages. Many school children could look with pride on healthy stands of timber they had helped replant in the "Tillamook burn" and in other areas where fires destroyed the timber.

In contrast to the attention given to public lands, the management of private Northwest timberlands was a lesser concern for Hatfield and other members of Congress. Landowners generally complied with state reforestation requirements. But public lands posed some difficult issues and it was essential for the federal government to address these issues.

A *private* landowner could prepare to harvest a parcel of timber, taking into account the cost of constructing roads and protecting water quality by adhering to restrictions on harvest near streams and rivers. But *federal* forest planners had to cover these management costs without the kinds of tax considerations that affect the management of private land. That meant Congress had to appropriate funds for pre-harvest management processes, including things like building roads for the harvest process, for fire control, and for recreation.

As a senator from a state with substantial amounts of federally managed timber, Hatfield found himself caught between the interests of the forest-products industry and those who wanted to put the brakes on all logging of public lands. Private landowners could see the merit in putting timber production on a cycle as short as 40 years, but federal foresters had been accustomed to utilizing harvest cycles twice as long. Senator Hatfield addressed some of these questions during his first speech on the Senate floor in 1967.

A decade later, Hatfield joined Senator Frank Church of Idaho in the passage of the National Forestry Management Act, a major piece of legislation that still guides federal forest-management practices. The bill required the Forest Service to develop specific management plans for each national forest that would allow multiple-use management while protecting the forests' "sustainability," an important new consideration in resource management.[9]

Saving the Wilderness

As aggravating as disputes over managing federal timber land for multiple uses could be, Hatfield found even more difficult the endless arguments about withdrawing federal timber lands from multiple use for indefinite preservation. At issue was the fate of "roadless" timberland which either had not been considered for timber harvest or had no networks of roads to facilitate harvest and access for other purposes.

CONCERN FOR GOD'S CREATION

The name "wilderness" came to be used for the roadless lands that by congressional action were withdrawn indefinitely from multiple use management. The word *wilderness* suggests parcels of land in very remote locations, and some of these pieces of land were indeed quite remote and untouched. But the main point was not their inaccessibility, but that they might by federal legislation be permanently removed from multiple uses.

While some hunters opposed designating the roadless lands for wilderness—they wanted access to the forests to hunt for deer, elk, and other wildlife—the much more important opposition voice came from the timber industry, which during Hatfield's time in the Senate enjoyed considerable political clout. Several large forest-products companies had their headquarters in Oregon and had no intention of standing quietly by while Congress designated more roadless parcels as wilderness. Most of the companies owned some forestland, but depended on harvests from public lands to keep their mills in operation.

Many citizen groups attentive to broader environmental issues such as clean air and water lined up against the timber companies. These groups saw the forests as part of a water-quality agenda and wanted to slow down timber harvests to reduce the loss of carbon dioxide from mature trees. Some anti-timber, pro-wilderness people expressed a deep reverence for the old-growth forests, and to help make their point, they began to speak about the "ancient" forests—a stretch in terminology as many species in the Northwest do not live nearly as long as the redwoods of northern California.

The hope for compromise between the polarized views seemed remote. On one side stood the pro-harvest advocates (the forest products companies, the communities that needed the jobs, and some unions). On the other side stood the anti-harvest and pro-wilderness groups, some of them moderate and some radical. It might have seemed easy enough for someone in Hatfield's position to identify and occupy a position exactly in the middle of these factions, since compromise is a time-honored strategy in political bargaining. Unfortunately, however, the two sides in the wilderness had no interest in splitting their differences. At least for bargaining purposes, they both had an "all-or-nothing" mentality.

As Hatfield spent time working for acceptable compromises on particular roadless areas, his stewardship ethic guided him. He saw no need to shut down all timber harvests as proposed by Harry Lonsdale—his opponent in his 1990 campaign for the Senate. For Hatfield, stewardship meant wise and sustained use of forests, and he felt comfortable with continued harvests of federal timber *if* the parcels could be restocked and *if* there was careful enforcement of federal rules on protecting streams and controlling soil erosion.

Hatfield regularly expressed his stewardship beliefs during debates about logging. He pointed out that lumber was the only renewable resource for home construction. The materials that make bricks, cement, plastics, and steel come from resources with finite supplies. He insisted that although land suitable for producing lumber is limited, good management can sustain production indefinitely.

Hatfield appealed to those who expressed concern about the poor to also support sustainability. Low-income people, he said, need the security and well-being that comes from having a comfortable and affordable home. With declining jobs in the forest-products industry, many were joining the ranks of the poor.

When Hatfield and other members of Congress visited forested areas of Siberia, Central America, and South America, those in the delegation felt appalled by the lack of sustainable management practices in these areas. The group saw vast areas in which trees had been cut down and not replaced. How could it be right, Hatfield argued, to shut down the multiple-use management of North American forests while pushing consumers toward the use of lumber from completely unregulated forests?[10]

In all his years of considering various wilderness proposals, Hatfield tried to maintain positive relationships with all those engaged in these issues. From time to time he sent staff members to communities near the areas under consideration for wilderness designation, and asked them to facilitate dialogue with the opposing parties. He asked staff members to actually set foot on each of the parcels, to get scientific counsel, and to continue to encourage discussions that could lead toward the more unusual and beautiful parcels being set aside as wilderness while the more commercially viable pieces could be kept for multiple use.[11]

As a result of Hatfield's years of political work, Congress set aside a total of two million acres of Oregon forests for wilderness and for other forms of protection, and he appropriately considered that to be an important part of his political legacy. Members of Congress from states with no public forests typically deferred to the local and regional members, so success in passing the bills required careful coordination among the members of the delegation from Northwest states.

As Hatfield looked back on this part of his career, he mentioned the Opal Creek Wilderness area—in the central Oregon Cascades—as one of the most impressive roadless areas he had helped protect. He spoke of the area as "an absolutely magnificent watershed with deep, old growth forests and water rushing and plunging over rocks—a great legacy for Oregon." He characterized his success on this legislation as "one of the most gratifying experiences" of his career.[12]

Battles over Water Use

Debates over water policies could be just as problematic as those over forests. In timber-policy debates, you could count on hearing from two sides of the argument. But in discussions about the use of Oregon's streams and rivers, many sides came to the debate.

At least three competing interest groups pressed for the protection of fish in the river, especially the prized Chinook and silver salmon. Native Americans sought to defend their treaty entitlements, seldom agreeing with the commercial fishing interests and those who fished recreationally. Still others competed for their share of the limited supplies of the water in the streams, including those wanting to maximize hydroelectric power production, others needing water for irrigation, and still others who counted on the rivers for municipal water supplies.

Hatfield approached Oregon's waterways much as he did the stewardship of forests. He considered rivers and streams part of God's treasured gifts to be used carefully. And he believed that wise use could assure their availability on a sustainable basis. But these views were sometimes difficult to apply to specific water controversies.

Throughout his years as governor, Hatfield rebuked politicians from California, Nevada, and Arizona who spoke as if Oregon's water supply exceeded its needs and that the state should divert major amounts to the south. Hatfield, in mock fierceness, spoke of California as a "thirsty camel" whose nose should never be allowed under the edges of Oregon's tent. Instead, said Hatfield, much of Oregon's dry eastern half could produce abundant crops, with proper irrigation systems. In the closing days of his time as governor, he helped get funding for a project of this type on the eastern edge of Oregon; 40 years later, it is still yielding impressive amounts of potatoes and other row crops.[13]

As hydroelectric dams began to go up on the Columbia River, Hatfield believed the multiple uses of these projects amply justified the expenditure of federal funds for their construction. Power production did not deplete the resource and the construction of navigation locks facilitated the movement of barges up and down the river, delivering grain and logs to ocean ports and returning with petroleum and other locally needed products. Hatfield judged the "fish ladders"—for moving salmon up and down the stream on their migratory pathways—to be well designed and reasonably effective. But Hatfield did have a concern that additional dams planned for one of the Columbia's major tributaries, the Snake River, would hinder the movement of salmon to their spawning areas. He felt pleased that those dams never got built.

In the later years of his public career, Hatfield disagreed with environmental groups that wanted most or all of the dams in Oregon and Washington removed. He had regularly supported the funding of research and development of clean and sustainable forms of electrical energy and he hated to see the loss of the dams that produced electricity with little or no harm to the environment. Supplies of "alternative energy" would not meet public needs, he argued, so giving up on hydropower would require shifting to "dirty" forms of power production, like coal, gas, and oil.

At one time Hatfield considered nuclear energy benign, but he later abandoned that position and expressed particular concern about the plutonium production reactors at Hanford in central Washington, not far from the Oregon border. Initially, Hatfield had supported nuclear-power production, but the nuclear-power plants had created a massive nuclear waste problem. He couldn't support building more of these nuclear-power plants to replace the safe and sustainable hydro plants.

Another possible replacement for the hydroelectric facilities might have been coal-fired power plants, such as the one built by a private power company in Oregon in the late 1970s. The plant, located well away from population centers, was expected to produce relatively few harmful emissions. But transporting coal from Colorado and Montana turned out to be very expensive and the plant remained unused for years after its construction. So Hatfield clung to a stewardship position regarding the state's waterways, based on careful use and respectful attentiveness to competing interests.[14]

Taking Stock

If Mark Hatfield were to return today to his favorite place on the Oregon coast to reflect on his efforts to protect Oregon's environment, he could feel some satisfaction. Through his efforts and in collaboration with many others, Congress established many new wilderness areas and gave protection to other naturally significant areas during his five terms in the Senate.

Most of the state's rivers are cleaner today than they were 50 years ago. Much of Oregon's coastal areas are protected from excessive development, and the Columbia River Gorge is now a national scenic area, assuring that its beauty will be protected in perpetuity. Hatfield always loved Oregon's natural beauty, and his efforts to guard that beauty flowed from his service to a God who calls humans to be careful stewards of the land.

12

CONSISTENT LIFE ETHIC

While many progressives applaud Hatfield's efforts to protect the environment, they have difficulty with one of his positions that they consider inconsistent with progressivism: his convictions about abortion.

A typical political liberal may see as a clash of values a strong commitment to peace/justice and a rejection of a woman's personal freedom to choose to discontinue a pregnancy. But Mark Hatfield didn't see a clash; he saw a consistent pair of values centered in the preciousness of human life. Hatfield, and other likeminded evangelical progressives also opposed capital punishment, expressed deep concern about gun violence, rejected euthanasia, and had great compassion for the victims of poverty and racism.[1]

A Concern for Life

Cardinal Joseph Bernardin, a prominent Catholic cleric, became one of the first to use the phrase "consistent life ethic." Bernardin had been the first general secretary of the National Conference of Catholic Bishops, then the archbishop of Cincinnati, and while serving as archbishop of Chicago rose to the position of cardinal. As head of the National Conference of Bishops' Ad Hoc Committee on War and Peace, he drafted a pastoral letter called "The Challenge of Peace: God's Promise and Our Response." The letter focused on the threat of nuclear war and the likelihood that many innocent civilians would die.

In a pair of lectures in 1984, Bernardin linked his concern about nuclear war with the threat to another category of innocent human victims: the unborn children who lost their lives through abortion.

People expected a Catholic priest to oppose abortion, but Bernardin went on to speak about a broad range of innocent victims besides those at risk from nuclear weapons and abortion. He included in his list the elderly persons in poor health, threatened by euthanasia; the poor and hungry, threatened by starvation; and those convicted of capital crimes, threatened by capital punishment.

Cardinal Bernardin called his ethical system a "seamless garment of life," using a reference from the Gospels that describes an article of clothing Jesus wore to the cross. Bernardin said, "Nuclear war threatens life on a previously unimaginable scale; abortion takes life daily on a horrendous scale; public executions are fast becoming weekly events in the most advanced technological society in history; and euthanasia is now openly discussed and even advocated."[2]

Only the more progressive Catholic leaders joined him in condemning such a broad range of threats against human life. For some Protestants, the thinking of a prominent Catholic cleric like Bernardin would have carried little weight. But Hatfield felt particularly drawn to Catholics like Bernardin and Mother Teresa, having married a Catholic and having a high regard for Mrs. Hatfield's family members who were Catholic. Among the staff members who shared Hatfield's Christian faith were those who were Catholic. In the later part of Hatfield's career in the Senate, staff members like Jim Towey reinforced his commitment to save the lives of the unborn. Towey had earlier expressed his Catholic values by working with Mother Teresa's ministry in India.

But Senator Hatfield found it difficult to find political support for the life-threatening issues discussed by Cardinal Bernardin. Some Democrats agreed with the importance of seeking peace and combating hunger and poverty, but few supported a pro-life position on abortion. And Republicans willing to support Hatfield on the abortion issue generally felt less concern about threats to life in the form of war, capital punishment, and poverty.

Mark Hatfield dealt with this dilemma throughout his political career. Although the abortion issue did not appear until his second term in the Senate, from the beginning of his national career he had to struggle with his own conscience and with skeptical constituents on the issues of war and capital punishment. Hatfield expressed his passion about the life-threatening practices of modern society as he reflected on his life and career in his memoirs: "I'm strongly against all these brutalities. We should wield no power to destroy human life in any way. I believe the hand of God is present in the creation of life, and humankind cannot take that divine power into our own hands. Ever."[3]

Capital Punishment

Hatfield had barely settled into the governor's office when he encountered the first of the life issues—capital punishment. He later called his first decision on capital punishment the most agonizing decision of his entire public life. Dealing with the pending execution of a murderer and trying to decide whether to exercise his power as governor to commute a sentence put him in a vise between his announced opposition to capital punishment and his responsibilities as governor to carry out the laws of the state.[4]

Capital punishment had been an issue during Hatfield's first campaign for governor in 1958, but his opponent, Democrat Robert Holmes, had taken a position against the death sentence identical to Hatfield's. Both supported a ballot measure to remove the death sentence in capital cases. What later complicated things for Hatfield occurred in a question period after a joint Holmes-Hatfield appearance hosted by the League of Women Voters. Hatfield dealt with the issue differently from the incumbent governor. Holmes said he would commute the sentences of all those on death row. Hatfield said he also opposed the death penalty, but that he would be obliged as the state's chief executive to carry out the will of the people and to act in harmony with the state constitution and statutes. He would look at the particulars of each case and would commute the sentences of those convicted only when judicial irregularities called into question the appropriateness of the conviction and sentencing.[5]

Unfortunately for Hatfield, the capital punishment repeal measure did not pass. Further complicating his legal and moral dilemma were the kinds of charges against those on death row. After Hatfield won the election, his new staff began to study the cases with the earliest scheduled execution dates.

The first case to actually come before Hatfield involved forty-year-old Leroy McGahuey, who had confessed to stabbing and bludgeoning his girlfriend and their twenty-three-month-old son. Governor Hatfield asked his legal counsel, Loren Hicks, to study the McGahuey

CONSISTENT LIFE ETHIC

case to determine if any aspects of the trial might be irregular enough to justify commutation. Hicks and Hatfield had been friends for many years and Hatfield felt sure that if grounds for commutation existed, Hicks would find it. But Hicks could identify no irregularities in the proceedings.[6]

Given those findings, Hatfield believed he had to let the process proceed toward execution, in keeping with the position he had taken earlier. Though he saw little likelihood of reversing himself, he kept that possibility open throughout the evening that led up to the scheduled execution at midnight. Close staff members, his wife, and a local pastor sat with him during the interminable hours and minutes before the scheduled death by lethal injection. A special telephone had been installed at the Hatfield home to permit him to call off the execution, and if he did not stop the proceedings, the warden would use the phone to report to him when the process had been completed.

Some Oregonians felt pleased with McGahuey's execution, but Governor Hatfield felt only sadness and regret. He said later, "Our vigil had ended, but would never be forgotten." He instructed one of his staff members to encourage the media to cover the event thoroughly. He wanted the public to feel the impact of taking a life. Six years later another initiative to eliminate capital punishment came before Oregon voters. Hatfield actively supported the measure and it passed by a substantial margin. Hatfield then did what Robert Holmes had said he would do even without the passage of the measure, that is, to commute the sentences of all those on death row. One of those commuted sentences belonged to Jeannace Freeman, a woman who killed her female lover's children in a brutal incident that included tossing the bodies into a deep canyon in central Oregon.[7] She would now spend the rest of her life in prison.

Voters later reinstated Oregon's death penalty, and since his retirement from office Hatfield has supported efforts for its repeal. Decades after the long wait for the call reporting McGahuey's execution, Hatfield wondered if he should have commuted the sentence. He accepted criticism for being inconsistent with his previous statements. He wondered if he should have invoked the "dictates of my conscience and my faith rather than my obligations to the majority will of the people, [that] I might rather render first unto God rather than unto Caesar."[8]

Hatfield did not find many opportunities to oppose the death penalty in the Senate. He did join forces, however, with Senator Paul Simon, Democrat from Illinois, in an effort to place restrictions on capital punishment. The measure would have prevented the imposition of the death penalty for mentally retarded individuals. In their presentations in Congress the two senators disputed the common position that the death sentence effectively deterred potential killers. And even if the argument of deterrence seemed persuasive to some, it still presumed perpetrators could rationally consider the consequences of their criminal actions—and the mentally impaired could not be expected to understand the implications of their actions.

In another initiative, Hatfield argued that citizens needed to become aware of the barbarity of executions. He introduced an amendment in the Senate that would have directed that executions be broadcast on television and radio. Other senators felt aghast at such a proposal, but the legislation harmonized with his position that the citizenry be fully aware of the details of taking a human life. He hoped that awareness would build support for ending capital punishment.[9]

When Does Life Begin?

Soon after Hatfield began his second term in the Senate, the human life issue that dominated public debate even more than capital punishment appeared on the political scene. In the *Roe v. Wade* and *Doe v. Bolton* cases in early 1973, the Supreme Court took the side of those who argued that a pregnant woman had the right to choose not to carry an unborn child to term, and that this right superseded the rights of the fetus.

According to the decision, most legislation on the subject violated a constitutional right to privacy under the due process clause of the Fourteenth Amendment. The court held that a pregnant woman could choose to have an abortion for any reason until the time the fetus became "viable," that is, able to sustain life on its own.

Applying his "consistent human life ethic" to this relatively new issue, Hatfield joined those in Congress who disagreed with the legal and moral reasoning involved in the Supreme Court cases. He cosponsored legislation—authored by conservative senator James Buckley from New York—that would have amended the constitution to ban all abortions except in cases of rape and the endangerment of the life of the pregnant woman.

Political prudence would have prescribed a lower profile on the abortion issue than what Hatfield took. While more Republicans felt drawn to the pro-life (anti-abortion) position than did Democrats, it soon became apparent that this was a "no-win" political issue for advocates of both positions. Oregon had many voters registered as Independents and Hatfield needed to attract their support, as well as that of Democrats, to stay in the Senate past his second term. While today we might assume Hatfield already had the progressive and liberal votes secured, the majority of Oregonians still did not support Hatfield's antiwar position. His pro-life position caused him even more difficulty because of the rigidity of many of the most adamant pro-life organizations and legislators.

While many members of Congress tried to determine where to come down on the abortion issue, Hatfield established a position different from most pro-life members of Congress. He disagreed with those who considered all birth control measures to involve the taking of life. Instead Hatfield asserted that life began at the time the embryo became attached or "implanted" in the mother's womb. That interval between conception and implantation allowed time for pills or procedures that would prevent implantation. Many of those who joined the pro-life movement, especially conservative Catholics, would not accept Hatfield's position on birth control and would support him only if the alternative were to back a pro-choice candidate.

Writing in a religious journal not long after the *Roe v. Wade* decision, Hatfield explained that he based his position on abortion on the necessity of protecting human life: "Abortion is a form of violence. That is the undeniable reality. It is the destruction of life. It furthers the dehumanization of life. It cheapens life." He warned that in the past a narrow definition of personhood had resulted in brutality on a massive scale, such as the enslavement of Africans and the slaughter of Jews. He challenged the notion that liberalizing abortion was essential to women's liberation, asserting that destroying life did not provide a valid pathway to liberation. Hatfield concluded the article with these words: "Let us believe in life. Let us nourish life. Let us commit ourselves to life."[10]

While weighing a woman's freedom to choose, Hatfield said he had to opt for the protection of human life. He didn't see the fetus as a "thing" or a "medical condition." This was a child, Hatfield argued, whose organs and limbs began forming a few weeks after implantation. He could not bring himself to think of it as something disposable. He couldn't come to terms with sacrificing a human life so a woman could get on with her life and a man could escape any further obligation for the pregnancy. Unconcerned about offending his liberal constituents, he pronounced that, "the humanization of mankind will never come through condoning the slaughter of unborn life."[11]

The Elusive Middle Ground

While those on the pro-life side of the debate felt pleased with statements like the one just cited, Hatfield regularly annoyed them by refusing to take a hard-line pro-life position. He insisted that any legislative proposal include the exceptions for rape and protecting the mother's life, as found in the first Buckley measure he cosponsored. Many pro-life groups opposed any exceptions in legislative remedies.

Hatfield also disagreed with the pro-choice position of such groups as Planned Parenthood, but he did agree with their support for sex education in the schools and their sponsorship of family-planning clinics. To speak positively about the work of Planned Parenthood, which he sometimes did, amounted to being in league with the devil, according to many pro-lifers.

Unlike some in Congress who supported pro-life legislation, Hatfield tried to keep the lines of communication open with pro-choice proponents. He acknowledged that he had met pro-choice advocates with Christian commitments as sincere as his own. Once when a group of pro-choice activists came to talk with him about supporting their side of the issue, Hatfield listened attentively, then asked if they felt he should violate his own conscience in order to back their position. They saw the point. This was a deeply held position for him, not just another political opinion. They expressed their respect for his deeply held views and left with a greater understanding of his moderate pro-life position.

Hatfield regularly joined his Republican pro-choice colleague from Oregon, Robert Packwood, in cosponsoring a resolution condemning violence directed against the persons and the property of the clinics that provided abortions. Hatfield supported measures to address the needs of women and their babies for nutritional and health assistance after the birth of the child and urged various groups to join in these efforts.[12]

Because of these moderate positions, Hatfield tangled more often with the rock-solid pro-life senators than he did with adamant pro-choice legislators such as Bob Packwood. When Hatfield first cosponsored the Buckley pro-life legislation, he made a point of articulating his own consistent-life-ethic position, which included opposition to capital punishment. Buckley, on the other hand, supported capital punishment.

While Hatfield chaired the Senate Appropriations Committee, he clashed regularly with his fellow pro-life senator, Jesse Helms, Republican from North Carolina. Becoming weary of Helms' frequent abortion "riders" on appropriation measures, Hatfield went to Helms, affirmed their mutual distaste for abortion, and then promised to do what he could to help get hearings on the abortion issue scheduled in appropriate venues.

Meanwhile, Hatfield said to Helms, it was essential for the Senate to move forward in processing the funding measures and to abstain from offering pro-life amendments. Helms agreed to more cautiously offer such amendments (or so Hatfield thought), but before long he offered yet another abortion amendment and refused to wait for hearings. Hatfield staffers discovered that senior members of the Helms staff persuaded him to give greater priority to his pro-life crusade than his promise to Hatfield. Violating an agreement with a senatorial colleague in this manner was a major violation of Senate culture, but an unpunishable one.[13]

Euthanasia

As part of his consistent life ethic, Hatfield did what he could to mobilize national resources for dealing with the suffering of those facing extreme poverty and starvation *(see chapter 10)*. On another of the consistent-life-ethic issues—euthanasia, or "death with dignity"—

Hatfield took the same "seamless-garment" position outlined by Cardinal Bernardin: It was wrong to terminate the lives of elderly persons suffering from painful and life-threatening conditions, or those with physical and mental problems.

Pro-euthanasia movements in England and the United States had arisen in the 1930s, but this position became difficult to sustain once the Nazis began systematically practicing euthanasia to rid Germany of those judged unable to make a contribution to society. The person most responsible for reviving the pro-euthanasia position during Hatfield's time in office was Dr. Jack Kevorkian, who in the 1990s began assisting terminal patients in taking their own lives. Dr. Kevorkian brought the "death-with-dignity" issue to Oregon soon after his first assisted suicide in Michigan, giving visibility to a local political effort that favored such actions under certain circumstances.

Oregon's initiative and referendum procedures have a long history in the state, and proponents of "death with dignity" used this means to pass an assisted suicide law in 1994. Voters cast more ballots on the measure than they did for governor that year, resulting in a close margin of victory. Three years later the Oregon legislature sent the issue back to the voters in the form of a repeal proposal. Hatfield did not normally take positions on state ballot measures after he retired from public life, but he made an exception in this case. In fact, he allowed his pro-repeal message to be used in the state's voter pamphlet. Despite his support, the repeal effort failed.

After his retirement, Hatfield spoke out more publicly and forcefully against his state's "assisted-suicide" legislation, calling it murder. He had worked hard to provide federal funding for medical research and for Oregon's medical school and teaching hospital, the Oregon Health & Science University. He believed the health-care profession could relieve the suffering of the sick and dying without making it legal to assist these patients in taking their own lives.[14]

Gun Violence

Hatfield also applied his consistent life ethic to his efforts to limit violence committed through the use of handguns and other small weapons. The U.S. Constitution's Second Amendment, which speaks of "the right of the people to keep and bear arms," has played a central role in the debate about firearms in the United States. And the political debate about its contemporary meaning has been a polarizing process.

What does the Second Amendment really mean? Hatfield insisted the amendment should be understood in the context of providing internal and national defense through the maintenance of a citizen militia. He had campaigned in Oregon's small towns and rural areas and knew how the state's many hunters felt loathe to have their ownership of guns restricted. While many hunters agreed that criminals not be allowed access to firearms, they didn't think restrictive measures should be applied to law-abiding sportsmen and competition shooters. Nor did they think that such restrictions would stop violent criminals from using guns they already owned or obtained illegally.

In his early career, Hatfield did not challenge the majority position in Oregon against gun control. But later in his Senate career, he began to support some gun-control measures. He decided that the cheap handguns typically used in crimes, the "Saturday-night specials," had no use in hunting or marksmanship and that their sale and purchase could and should be restricted. He also concluded that the semi-automatic and automatic weapons should be put in a different category from the rifles used for hunting and marksmanship. He argued that systems of technology could appropriately track the sale of weapons in order to make it less likely that firearms would wind up in the hands of those with criminal records.

By taking this stand, Hatfield knowingly incurred the wrath of the National Rifle Association (the NRA), who, like the pro-life forces, wanted members of Congress to back their positions completely. By the end of Hatfield's political career, the NRA had become one of the strongest public-policy groups of any kind in the United States—and although it had large sums of money to use for and against political candidates, it was not a force in his last campaign.[15]

A Coherent Position

The various political positions that grew out of Mark Hatfield's consistent life ethic reflect a coherence in the evangelical progressivism that shaped his political thought and actions. He took no joy in struggling with the hard cases of capital punishment. He did not go looking for unpopular issues when he decided to take a stand against the Vietnam

War and against nuclear weapons. He had no political death wish when he decided to oppose the Supreme Court's broadened parameters of abortion.

What do these and other consistent-life-ethic issues have in common? They all focus on the sacredness of human life. Advocates of such a philosophy willingly declare the protection of human life to be a moral absolute, and Hatfield consistently took that stand, without hesitation.

CONCLUDING REFLECTIONS

In the year 2000 I was getting ready to return to my alma mater, George Fox University, to serve in an administrative position. I received an e-mail from one of my future colleagues asking if I would co-teach a course with Senator Hatfield, who had been a visiting professor at George Fox since his retirement from the Senate four years before.

I replied something like this: "I will most certainly do it, whatever the topic. And if necessary, I will gladly pay for the privilege." I knew it would be an honor and a challenge to co-teach a course with Hatfield. And I thought it would be amusing as his new academic dean to become his "boss" after ten years of enjoying working for him.

On one of the last days he taught at George Fox, Hatfield sat down with a student who wanted his guidance in considering a career in politics. He did so with the same compassion, focus, and sensitivity that he had given to hundreds of other such young people at George Fox and at other universities and high schools. Few of those he counseled probably will find their way into political careers, but Hatfield encouraged this student to remain faithful in exercising his gifts and to follow God's leading, whether it should be in the direction of politics or in some very different pursuit.

The advice he gave to the student largely echoed one of the closing paragraphs in his memoir *Against the Grain.* That passage reads like something out of the biblical book of Proverbs:

> Define your own spiritual commitment. Encourage your conscience. Use loving spirituality to infuse your personal, public, and political acts. Take advantage of spiritual stewardship when dealing with political issues such as the environment, the needs of humans, the dangers of war. Demonstrate commitment by actions which address the needs of humans, not actions which destroy. Find like-minded friends, encourage one another and build support as you

would a living cell. Your spirit will multiply as naturally as the cells within us all.[1]

While working on this project I spoke in class about another of my favorite people, William Wilberforce. I described some of the moral, spiritual, and intellectual qualities that Wilberforce and Hatfield had in common. I also talked about their willingness to stand alone, their frustration with ending up on the short end of so many votes, and their discomfort with occupying the unusual and uncomfortable place of an evangelical progressive. As I spoke I realized again how important it is for stories about these two men to be known and understood.

Wilberforce has enjoyed a rediscovery in recent years and has appropriately become a role model for evangelical progressives in politics. Mark Hatfield is one of a few politicians deserving consideration along with Wilberforce as an example of moral and spiritual commitment in the messy world of politics. It is my hope that young people today—those who were very young when Hatfield completed his work in the Senate—will come to know and appreciate this remarkable man and his brand of evangelical progressivism.

ENDNOTES

Preface

1. Jim Wallis, "The Courage of Conviction: An Interview with Sen. Mark Hatfield," *Sojourners,* September/October 1996, 28.

1. The Evangelical Experience

1. Mark O. Hatfield, *Conflict and Conscience* (Waco, TX: Word, 1971), 98.

2. Mark Hatfield interview, transcript, Hatfield Oral History Collection, Oregon Historical Society (hereafter cited as OHS), Portland, Oregon, 15, 19.

3. Mark Hatfield interview, OHS, 46; Doug Coe interview, OHS, 7.

4. Hatfield, *Conflict and Conscience,* 96.

5. Robert Eells and Bartell Nyberg, *Lonely Walk: The Life of Senator Mark Hatfield* (Chappaqua, NY: Christian Herald, 1979), 28; Hatfield, *Conflict and Conscience,* 97.

6. Hatfield, *Conflict and Conscience,* 97.

7. Mark O. Hatfield, as told to Diane N. Solomon, *Against the Grain* (Ashland, OR: White Cloud Press, 2001), 242.

8. Eells and Nyberg, *Lonely Walk,* 30.

9. Doug Coe interview, OHS, 4-11.

10. Ibid., 12.

11. Ibid., 13-17.

12. Lon Fendall, *To Live Free: William Wilberforce—Experiencing the Man, the Mission, and the Legacy* (Uhrichsville, OH: Barbour Books, 2007), 69, 75.

13. James M. Houston, ed., *Real Christianity Contrasted With the Prevailing Religious System* (Portland, OR: Multnomah, 1982), xv-xvii.

14. Fendall, *To Live Free,* 79-90.

15. Hatfield, *Conflict and Conscience,* 158.

16. Doug Coe interview, OHS, 17-20.

17. Hatfield, *Conflict and Conscience*, 22, 98-99.

2. Evangelicalism and Progressivism

1. Walter Russell Mead, "God's Country?" *Foreign Affairs,* September/October 2006, 24-43.

2. Tony Campolo, *Speaking My Mind: The Radical Evangelical Prophet Tackles the Tough Issues Christians Are Afraid to Face* (Nashville, TN: W Publishing Group, 2004), 231-232.

3. Hatfield, *Conflict and Conscience*, 15.

4. Hatfield, *Conflict and Conscience*, 24-25.

5. Mark Hatfield, *Between a Rock and a Hard Place* (Waco, TX: Word, 1976), 23-25.

6. Eells and Nyberg, *Lonely Walk*, 73-74, 142.

7. Hatfield, *Against the Grain*, 146-147.

8. Wes Granberg-Michaelson, e-mail message to author, August 22, 2007.

9. Wallis, "The Courage of Conviction," 26.

10. Jim Wallis, *God's Politics: Why the Right Gets It Wrong and the Left Doesn't Get It* (New York, NY: HarperOne, 2005), xxi.

11. Wes Michaelson interview, OHS, A1- A38.

12. Charles Colson, *Born Again* (New York, NY: Bantam, 1976).

13. Hatfield, *Between a Rock and a Hard Place*, 26-27; Wes Michaelson interview, OHS, B41.

14. Hatfield, *Against the Grain*, 66.

15. David Hardin, interview of Richard Halverson by David Hardin, www.30goodminutes.org/csec/sermon/halverson_3303.htm (accessed July 8, 2008).

3. A Republican Progressive

1. M. Kent Jennings and Richard G. Niemi, "TheTransmission of Political Values From Parent to Child," in Jack Dennis, *Socialization to Politics: A Reader* (New York, NY: John Wiley and Sons, 1973), 330-331.

2. Mark O. Hatfield, *Not Quite So Simple* (New York, NY: Harper & Row, 1968), 55.

3. Hatfield, *Against the Grain*, 22-23.

4. Hatfield, *Not Quite So Simple*, 10; Hatfield, *Against the Grain*, 28.

5. Hatfield, *Not Quite So Simple*, 10-11.

6. Ibid., 13.

7. Ibid., 13-15.

8. Mark Hatfield interview, OHS, 26.

9. David M. Kennedy, *Freedom From Fear: The American People in Depression and War, 1929-1945* (New York, NY: Oxford University Press, 1999), 91-95.

10. Cited in Hatfield, *Not Quite So Simple*, 29.

11. Hatfield, *Not Quite So Simple*, 82.

12. Hatfield, *Against the Grain*, 8.

13. Hatfield, *Not Quite So Simple*, 21-22.

14. *Portland Oregonian,* May 4, 1956, cited in Eells and Nyberg, *Lonely Walk*, 34.

15. Hatfield, *Not Quite So Simple*, 90-95.

16. Eells and Nyberg, *Lonely Walk*, 49.

17. Ibid., 50.

18. Hatfield, *Against the Grain*, 95.

19. Ibid., 94.

20. Ibid., 132-133.

21. Mark O. Hatfield, "Richard Nixon for President," *Christianity and Crisis,* July 22, 1968, 165-166; Wes Granberg-Michaelson, e-mail message to author, August 15, 2007.

22. Eells and Nyberg, *Lonely Walk*, 63-64.

23. Wes Granberg-Michaelson, e-mail message to author, August 15, 2007.

24. Eells and Nyberg, *Lonely Walk*, 59.

25. Hatfield, *Against the Grain*, 128-129.

26. Norman Mailer, *Miami and the Siege of Chicago* (New York, NY: The New American Library, 1968), 69-70.

27. Hatfield, *Against the Grain*, 130.

28. Ibid., 130-131.

29. Wes Granberg-Michaelson, e-mail message to author, August 15, 2007.

30. Hatfield, *Against the Grain*, 148; Eells and Nyberg, *Lonely Walk*, 15.

31. Hatfield, *Against the Grain*, 148.

32. *Portland Oregonian,* October 26, 1978, cited in Eells and Nyberg, *Lonely Walk*, 165.

4. Walking the Talk

1. Doug Coe interview, OHS, 7.

2. Mark Hatfield interview, OHS, 3.

3. James M. Houston, ed., *Real Christianity*, xvii.

4. Hatfield, *Conflict and Conscience*, 151-153.

5. Ibid., 157.

6. Eells and Nyberg, *Lonely Walk*, 39.

7. Hatfield, *Between a Rock and a Hard Place*, 15, 27.

8. Marty Gold interview, OHS, 56; Tom Getman, e-mail message to the author, June 24, 2007.

9. Tom Getman, e-mail message to the author, June 24, 2007.

10. Doug Coe interview, OHS, 61.

11. Walt Evans interview, OHS, 110, 123.

12. Hatfield, *Against the Grain,* 184.

13. Leslie Maitland Werner stories in *New York Times*, August 8-20, 1984.

14. *New York Times*, August 10, 1984.

15. Leslie Maitland Werner, *New York Times*, April 19, 1987.

16. Hatfield, *Against the Grain*, 122.

17. Richard L. Berke, "For Hatfield, a Shining Image Tarnished by Ethics Charges," *New York Times,* June 6, 1991.

18. Sharon Lafraniere and Bill Mcalister, "Oregon's 'St. Mark'—Hatfield's Career is Sullied Over Conflict of Interest," *The Seattle Times,* May 31, 1991.

19. Christopher Hanson, "Ethics Issues May Undo Once-Invincible Hatfield," *The Seattle Times,* June 6, 1991; "Hatfield Rebuked for Failing to Report Gifts," *The Seattle Times,* August 13, 1992.

5. Relationships Matter

1. Mason Drukman, *Wayne Morse: A Political Biography* (Portland, OR: Oregon Historical Society Press, 1997), 1-7.

2. Marty Gold interview, OHS, 114-119.

3. Hatfield, *Between a Rock and a Hard Place*, 17-18; Tom Getman, e-mail message to the author, June 24, 2007.

4. Hatfield, *Between a Rock and a Hard Place*, 18-19.

5. Hatfield, *Against the Grain*, 168-187.

6. Drukman, *Wayne Morse*, 186-187; Mark Hatfield interview, OHS, 292.

7. Hatfield, *Against the Grain*, 108.

8. Hatfield, *Against the Grain*, 109; Drukman, *Wayne Morse*, 439.

9. Wes Granberg-Michaelson interview, OHS, 51.

10. Hatfield, *Against the Grain*, 109; Drukman, *Wayne Morse*, 364.

11. Ibid., 169.

12. Ibid., 170-171.

13. Drukman, *Wayne Morse*, 311-316; Wes Granberg- Michaelson, e-mail message to the author, August 15, 2007.

14. Tom Imeson interview, OHS, 55.

15. Hatfield, *Against the Grain*, 173.

16. Ibid., 174.

17. Ibid., 177.

18. Ibid., 174.

19. Mark Hatfield interview, OHS, 120-122; Warne Nunn obituary, *The Oregonian*, June 21, 2007.

20. Janet Lamos, correspondence with the author, May 11, 2007.

21. Jenna Dorn interview, OHS, 77-82.

22. Hatfield, *Against the Grain*, 123; Richard Halverson interview, OHS, 4.

23. Tom Imeson interview, OHS, 91-93.

24. Walter Evans interview, OHS, 70.

6. Seeking Peace and Justice

1. Hope Kauffman Lind, *Apart and Together: Mennonites in Oregon and Neighboring States, 1876-1976* (Scottsdale, PA: Herald Press, 1990), 164-169.

2. Hatfield, *Against the Grain*, 37-41.

3. Ibid., 42.

4. Ibid., 44-45.

5. Ibid., 44.

6. Ibid., 200.

7. Hatfield, *Between a Rock and a Hard Place*, 37.

8. Ibid., 135.

9. Ibid., 135-140.

10. Ibid., 141-146.

11. John Paul Lederach, *Building Peace: Sustainable Reconciliation in Divided Societies* (Washington, D.C.: United States Institute of Peace Press, 1997).

12. Tom Getman, e-mail to the author, July 9, 2007. Hatfield explained to a former member of his staff that he had decided to announce his support for the war in part after communicating with officials from the Bush administration, who assured him that Saddam Hussein was part of the 9/11 attack and was prepared to attack the United States with nuclear weapons.

13. Wes Granberg-Michaelson, speech given at North Park University, April 26, 2007.

14. Ibid.

15. Edward Kennedy and Mark O. Hatfield, *Freeze! How You Can Help Prevent Nuclear War*, (New York, NY: Bantam,1982).

16. Wes Granberg-Michaelson, e-mail message to the author, August 22, 2007.

17. Hatfield, *Not Quite So Simple*, 268.

18. Hatfield, *Conflict and Conscience*, 41-42.

7. Butter or Guns

1. Hatfield, *Conflict and Conscience*, 43.

2. Hatfield quote in *Congressional Record* 135, no. 107 (August 2, 1989), www.nuclearfiles.org/menu/key-issues/ethics/issues/political/hatfield_congressional-record-statement.htm (accessed July 7, 2008).

3. James M. Houston, ed., *Real Christianity*, xxiii.

4. Hatfield, *Not Quite So Simple*, 166-168.

5. Ibid., 272.

6. Hatfield, *Against the Grain*, 139.

7. Ibid., 141.

8. Ibid., 230-232.

9. Ibid., 232.

10. Ibid., 232-233.

11. Eells and Nyberg, *Lonely Walk*, 160.

12. Rick Rolf interview, OHS, B5, 6.

13. Hatfield, *Against the Grain*, 212.

8. A Governor and the Vietnam War

1. Arlie Schardt, William A. Rusher, and Mark O. Hatfield, *Amnesty? The Unsettled Question of Vietnam* (Croton-on-Hudson, NY: Sun River Press, 1973), 109.

2. Hatfield, *Not Quite So Simple*, 153-154.

3. Hatfield, *Between a Rock and a Hard Place*, 23-24.

4. Hatfield, *Conflict and Conscience*, 28-29.

5. Hatfield, *Not Quite So Simple*, 155-156.

6. Eells and Nyberg, *Lonely Walk*, 56.

7. Hatfield, *Against the Grain*, 97.

8. Ibid., 100.

9. Hatfield, *Not Quite So Simple*, 160-161.

9. The Vietnam War in the Senate

1. Hatfield, *Not Quite So Simple*, 162; Hatfield, *Against the Grain,* 102-103.

2. Hatfield, *Not Quite So Simple*, 163.

3. "Monsoon Season," *Time*, November 4, 1966, 32.

4. Hatfield, *Against the Grain*, 107.

5. Hatfield, *Not Quite So Simple*, 169.

6. Ibid., 173-174.

7. Ibid., 175-177.

8. Wes Michaelson interview, OHS, A45; Hatfield, "Richard Nixon for President."

9. Hatfield, *Against the Grain*, 134.

10. Ibid.; Eells and Nyberg, *Lonely Walk*, 64.

11. Wes Michaelson interview, OHS, A23-A38.

12. Wes Michaelson interview, OHS, B13; Hatfield, *Against the Grain*, 129.

13. Eells and Nyberg, *Lonely Walk*, 66.

14. Ibid., 67.

15. Wes Michaelson interview, OHS, B15-B16.

16. Wes Granberg-Michaelson, e-mail message to the author, August 15, 2007.

17. Hatfield, *Between a Rock and a Hard Place*, 13-16.

18. Wallis, "The Courage of Conviction," 26-27.

19. Hatfield, *Between a Rock and a Hard Place*, 30.

20. Hatfield, *Conflict and Conscience*, 21-22; Eells and Nyberg, *Lonely Walk,* 76.

21. Wes Granberg-Michaelson, e-mail message to the author, August 15, 2007. Because of Hatfield's close alliance with McGovern on the Vietnam War issue, McGovern had Hatfield on a short list as choices for the vice presidency. This was not made public at the time; it would not have been acceptable to party leaders; and it would have forced Hatfield to drop out of his own campaign. Another opportunity Hatfield passed up in the 1972 presidential year was a proposal that he enter the New Hampshire primary as a Republican peace candidate, running against Nixon.

22. Tom Imeson interview, OHS, 87.

23. Rick Rolf interview, OHS, A120.

24. Schardt, Rusher, and Hatfield, *Amnesty? The Unsettled Question of Vietnam*, 107-148; Eells and Nyberg, *Lonely Walk*, 123-125.

25. Wes Michaelson interview, OHS, C4; Wes Granberg-Michaelson, e-mail to the author, August 22, 2007.

10. Global Hunger and Poverty

1. Wallis, *God's Politics*, 212.

2. Hatfield, *Conflict and Conscience*, 15, 39, 41.

3. James M. Houston, ed., *Real Christianity*, xxiv.

4. Hatfield, *Conflict and Conscience*, 43, 53.

5. Eells and Nyberg, *Lonely Walk*, 135.

6. Hatfield, *Against the Grain*, 44-45.

7. Ibid., 161-163; Tom Getman, e-mail message to the author, July 19, 2007.

8. Hatfield, *Between a Rock and a Hard Place*, 197.

9. Hatfield, *Not Quite So Simple*, 70.

10. Hatfield, *Conflict and Conscience*, 59.

11. Hatfield, *Between a Rock and a Hard Place,* 173-180.

12. Hatfield, *Conflict and Conscience*, 30-31.

13. James M. Houston, ed., *Real Christianity*, xxiv.

14. Hatfield, *Against the Grain*, 208-209.

15. Hatfield, *Between a Rock and a Hard Place*, 198-202.

16. Eells and Nyberg, *Lonely Walk*, 135.

17. Hatfield, *Between a Rock and a Hard Place*, 201-202.

18. Wes Granberg-Michaelson, e-mail message to the author, August 15, 2007; Eells and Nyberg, *Lonely Walk*, 136-138.

19. Eells and Nyberg, *Lonely Walk*, 135-136.

20. Ibid., 138.

21. Hatfield, *Between a Rock and a Hard Place*, 105-106.

22. Eells and Nyberg, *Lonely Walk*, 136.

23. Festo Kivengere, *I Love Idi Amin* (Old Tappan, NJ: F.H. Revell Co., 1977).

24. Hatfield, *Against the Grain*, 196.

25. Hatfield, *Between a Rock and a Hard Place*, 212.

11. Concern for God's Creation

1. Wallis, *God's Politics*, 353.

2. Hatfield, *Against the Grain*, 218.

3. Hatfield, *Between a Rock and a Hard Place*, 185.

4. Ibid., 186, 191.

5. Also see Revelation 11:18 for a harsh prophecy of what awaits those who "destroy the earth."

6. Hatfield, *Between a Rock and a Hard Place*, 195-196.

7. Eells and Nyberg, *Lonely Walk*, 117.

8. Hatfield, *Not Quite So Simple*, 133-134.

9. Hatfield, *Against the Grain*, 216.

10. Ibid., 219-220.

11. Jenna Dorn interview, OHS, 57.

12. Hatfield, *Against the Grain*, 216.

13. Hatfield, *Not Quite So Simple*, 135-137.

14. Hatfield, *Against the Grain*, 216.

12. Consistent Life Ethic

1. Wallis, *God's Politics*, 297-306.

2. Joseph Cardinal Bernardin, "A consistent Ethic of Life: Continuing the Dialogue," The William Wade Lecture Series, St. Louis University, March 11, 1984, www.priestsforlife.org/magisterium/bernardinwade.html (accessed July 7, 2008).

3. Hatfield, *Against the Grain*, 89.

4. Hatfield, *Between a Rock and a Hard Place*, 111.

5. Hatfield, *Against the Grain*, 82-83.

6. Ibid., 84-85.

7. Ibid., 86-88.

8. Hatfield, *Between a Rock and a Hard Place*, 111-112.

9. Hatfield, *Against the Grain*, 88-89.

10. Mark O. Hatfield, "Abortion: A Legislator Speaks," *The Reformed Journal*, September 1973, 11-14.

11. Eells and Nyberg, *Lonely Walk*, 95-96.

12. Wallis, "The Courage of Conviction," 29; Janet Lamos, correspondence with the author, July 11, 2007; Hatfield, *Against the Grain*, 90.

13. Hatfield, *Against the Grain*, 90-91; Wes Granberg-Michaelson, e-mail to the author, August 15, 2007; Tom Getman, e-mail to the author, July 19, 2007.

14. Hatfield, *Against the Grain*, 9.

15. Ibid., 91.

Concluding Reflections

1. Hatfield, *Against the Grain*, 245-246.

INDEX

Fulbright, J. William, 87, 111, 116
Fuller Theological Seminary, 13

Gandhi, Mahatma, 76
Goldwater, Barry, 31-33, 102
Goodell, Charles, 119
Graham, Billy, 37, 80
Granberg-Michaelson, Wes, 16-18, 21, 65, 80, 115, 117, 123, 131
Gravel, Mike, 122
Green, Edith, 30, 121
Gunnar, Peter, 38

Halverson, Richard, 20, 67
Hatch, Orrin, 63
Hatfield, Antoinette, 19, 48-50
Hatfield, Charles Dolen, 2, 24, 94
Hatfield, Dovie Odom, 2, 23, 42
Hatfield (Keller), Elizabeth, 52
Hatfield, Visko, 52
Helms, Jesse, 91-92, 158
Hendrickson, Margie, 50
Hicks, Loren, 64, 153-154
Hiroshima, 73-74, 79, 97, 127
Holderman, James, 51-52
Holmes, Robert, 153-154
Hoover, Herbert, 25-27, 126, 134
Hughes, Harold, 18-19, 42, 116-117
Humphrey, Hubert, 34, 103, 114, 134
Huss, Walter, 39-40

Imeson, Tom, 68
Indochina, 97-102, 127
Iwo Jima, 72-73, 97

Jackson, Glenn, 58
Javits, Jacob, 32
Jennings, Peter, 37
John Birch Society, 32, 102
Johnson, Lyndon, 102-104, 108-109, 118
Jordan, B. Everett, 117

Kennedy, John F., 100, 102
Kennedy, Robert, 109
Kennedy, Ted, 80
Kevorkian, Jack, 159
King, Coretta Scott, 80

9 781594 980152